Falling into Place

Also by Jane Routh
published by smith|doorstop Books

Circumnavigation
Teach Yourself Mapmaking
The Gift of Boats

Falling into Place

JANE ROUTH

smith|doorstop

Published 2014 by
smith|doorstop Books
The Poetry Business
Bank Street Arts
32-40 Bank Street
Sheffield S1 2DS
www.poetrybusiness.co.uk

ISBN 978-1-906613-97-6

British Library Cataloguing-in-Publication Data.
A catalogue record for this book is available from
the British Library.

Typeset in Garamond by Catherine Dodds
Cover design by Catherine Dodds
Cover image: Bowland Knotts © Graham Cooper –
www.forestofbowlandimages.com
Black and white photographs © Jane Routh

smith|doorstop Books is a member of Inpress,
www.inpressbooks.co.uk. Distributed by Central Books Ltd.,
99 Wallis Road, London E9 5LN.

The Poetry Business is an Arts Council
National Portfolio Organisation

for those who come after

CONTENTS

OPENING

It was dark when I left the Village Institute. And cold. Home was only a half hour drive but as soon as I turned inland from the bay I was in fog, thick swathes of it.

In the odd clearing you could see how it swirled and clung to the ground. The road followed the rivers along their valleys and the fog followed the rivers: it would be over an hour before I crossed the Roeburn, then the Hindburn, and changed down into second for the hill. Half way up I was suddenly in a clear, dark night.

Turning off the headlights turned on the sky. Stars. Stars crowded the sky, not just the stars of a routine moonless night, not just the aerial fog of the Milky Way, but stars beyond those and deeper and beyond those, filling every space with a depth of glitter. It was such an extraordinarily unfamiliar sky above this well-known hill: so many, such bright stars, I didn't even think to look for The Plough. I'd seen skies like this before, but only in remote places like north Ardnamurchan, miles from any light source. How could the air be as clear as this at home? I stood outside the house until my neck hurt and I was chilled through.

It's three in the morning when I wake, connecting fog and stars. The nearest town's fifteen miles distant but there's always an orange loom above it in the south west sky. It wasn't there tonight. No lightness near the horizon above the village to the east either. That low-lying thick fog trapped the light pollution, so that up here above it, I'd seen stars as pre-electric generations saw them.

I'd passed only three or four cars on the way home; had anyone else worked out what had happened? Would I remember this sky? Sitting up, feeling for a pencil, I resolve (for the umpteenth time) to keep notes. Not exactly a journal, more a gathering of what I wouldn't want to lose from, say, February, so I could say *how February feels*. This time, the resolve sticks. The notebook stays open.

CENSUS

The full extent of your holding to be outlined in red. Holding. I like that word: *they* would have used it, the men who drained the moor, built the cops, planted them with holly and thorn. It's different from 'owning' land, just holding it, just trying to manage it for your lifetime, working with what *they* did, then passing it on. This isn't about vocabulary, it's about soul – reciprocally,   I am   held.

The land's wet: heavy clay. Cattle have to be kept clear in the winter months, though a gentle southerly aspect to all the fields means frosts quickly burn off. ***Seasonal land, other arrangements.*** The two best meadows, with water troughs and road access are let for hay and winter grazing for sheep. ***Fowls and other poultry.*** Geese have the rest – far more than they 'need'; I have to mow their pastures in summer.

The southern boundary's the rocky bed of the River Hindburn. After rain on the moors, it's up and brown and frothy with overfalls. After a dry spell you can usually find somewhere (an old ford?) to wade across. ***Grassland etc, category G14.*** The valley's so steep it can only be wooded – the seven acres of ASNW was only £500 when I bought it – too steep, too inaccessible for anything commercial. (Ancient Semi-Natural Woodland. Pre 1640 I think the date is for ASNW.) Old elm and hazel coppice, elm now dead (Dutch elm disease 1995 onwards) leaving a poor mix of ash (the only tree that does well on these soils) birch, alder, sycamore, a few cherry and one or two oaks (sessile). Some elm I felled before it died – and hey, there are new shoots (not yet of beetle-able size) – is this survival?

Without cattle and sheep to poach it, the mud of the Old Wood's returned to woodland floor, this week brilliant green and stinking with wild garlic (soon to be starry), but there'll be bluebells next month. Patches of primroses in the gullies, violets if you look more closely. Early purple orchids. There are rare things too, tiny insignificant green things that excite botanists. Wood spiders, stuff I don't know about. There's very little regen though: too many roe deer browsing new shoots.

The first time I saw a deer here was about 1990. Now I see them every time I set foot outside (quietly, I mean). A few years back, the first buzzard. Now they're circling every day, using the chimney for thermals. Badgers, too. This is bad news. There always was a goodly number. Protected, their populations have exploded. Pressure on territory. They can't dig here (too wet) but they dine here – grubbing up pignuts until the field looks ploughed. Taking every last goose egg. Not so far this year any of my beautiful birds, though last winter they took five. Goodbye to all ground-nesters?

The eastern boundary's a deep un-named gill that runs into the river, dries in hot summers. In that corner between beck and river, a small field slopes so steeply it's never had fertiliser, retains all its old flora – wild carrot giving it a white froth in May before summer's purples of hardheads and betony. Long-tailed tits hang out here in the winter, swinging on the birch catkins. All the other fields are level enough to have been worked, to have been fertilised into monocultures. Gradually, gradually things may come back. I found four marsh orchids last year.

The north boundary's the first area I planted – a long thin wood that calls itself the Little Wood. Lots of the white willows have blown over. Only ash seems to hold on in wet ground. We've logged, brashed and re-planted with young ash and alder. *Nursery stock etc. category D10.* I grow all my own whips now, no point buying-in and anyway it's better for the gene pool not to. When I first put them in my neighbour Doreen then aged seventy said what was the point of a field full of little sticks: that's not a wood. She walks the woods now more than I do, with her terrier, rabbiting.

So. West is where the two better meadows are and from there you look down the valley to where the Hindburn joins the Roeburn and down the Lune to the coast. The wind blows up from the Irish Sea. Sometimes it feels as though this building is the first thing it hits inland. The patches of trees I've put in, thirty- to forty-footers now some of them, must break it though. You can't ever properly imagine how big a tree will be ten years later, I mean the trees you put in as whips that leg it past big nursery standards within three years.

I'll be buried not quite in the centre but near, where Great Robins Close (one of the old field names) starts to slope down to the Old Wood, by some of the better trees I've put in (including a wild crab apple I grew from seed that's transfigured by a million early blossoms every year), with the view upstream to the fells, the hare dashing around, the curlews calling... ***Details of others working on the holding, casual.*** Ken knows where to dig the hole; it's important not to disturb the land drains. I don't hold with cremations, the pollution. Better to feed microbes, worms, become grass. Hares prefer the new shoots after grass has been cut, about three inches long.

FEBRUARY

February filldyke, my mother always used to say. I don't know whether the dykes this month is supposed to fill are just Fenland dykes, or whether ditches all over the country overflow.

Born in the Fens in 1917, the language she heard and learned in childhood would have been wholly local. But as a child, you've no idea your language is local – some words even particular to your own family – until you meet other ways of speaking. 'Skerrick', I said the other day, only to discover this word of hers isn't universally understood. My mother would have started to lose her local speech when she went to secondary school in Sleaford, the High School intent on making a lady out of her. Or at least a teacher.

The beginning of WWII took her to a town; she would have heard radio language then. Television, when she was 40. By the end of her life I'm not sure whether you'd have been able to tell where she was from – certainly her brothers and sisters had broad Lincolnshire accents in comparison. But maybe vocabulary's more deeply ingrained, and phrases.

Filldyke doesn't describe what actually happens in February: the month's considerably drier – by about a third – than January if you look at rainfall statistics. It's a countryman's prayer rather than a forecast: *may dykes be full* before things start to grow. No filldyke this year at least, the land drier underfoot after a winter of frosts than it was all last summer. Snowdrops are at their best now, spilling out of hedgerows and down banks wherever there was an old farmstead – as much a marker of human habitation as nettles in summer.

Today, 22nd, is a friend's birthday, one that's easy to remember as this is the day curlews return inland from the coast. I've been listening. I've not actually heard one yet, though I did last year, right on time in spite of the fact that it was horribly wet. I thought I could have heard one yesterday, distant, plaintive. The point about February is that I keep going outdoors. I lost all interest in the garden (again) over the winter, and now the merest brightness has me outside, clearing armfuls of birch twigs that break off throughout the winter, mulching the hellebore buds that are thrusting up, despairing at precocious weedlings. *February saprising*, I'd say.

Sap rising literally, too. Last year I cut a small overhanging branch from a 25-year-old birch trunk, returning after a while as I was puzzled by something moving. It was a fast drip of liquid from the cut. I collected half a pint and sipped cautiously – though it must have been one of the most well-filtered waters I've ever drunk. Fermented, I think it would have tasted like retsina. Birch wine! So that's what it is. I'd also seen sycamore weep, felled at this time of year: I remember one pouring out stalagmites of ice in the cold – so many gallons of sap, and not destined to go up into leaves to evaporate, only rising to swell the promise of bud.

Maybe you notice moments of winter warmth more, simply by contrast with the wet and cold. I've a clear memory of sitting outside for lunch one 1st February and feeling some warmth on the shoulder of my coat. I'm sure of the date (though I've had to track the year by looking for a poem I wrote: 2005) because we saw nine buzzards circling above us. Ken always says *Look higher* when we hear distant mewling but haven't yet spotted the birds, and he's right: they're usually directly overhead. Those nine were, but very high, sweeping in vast circles up there. We decided they'd gathered in a sort of parliament to stake out the territory for the season and after that we were back to the usual pair working the valley.

A couple of years before, I'd noted the first wild daff open in the wood on Valentine's Day. It was cold, but the sun was out and 'I can't stay in any more' I wrote. February has a *feel* to it. I even projected this awareness on to fellow creatures. There was 'an odd feeling to the day; creatures have been wandering about, oddly, unseasonably'. In the morning there was a weasel strolling along to and under the side gate, and then messing around in the clematis netting. Next a stoat flipped and rolled under the front gate, trotted along the edge of the flower bed and went out under the side gate where the weasel had gone. He was soon back, and idled around on the lawn, not quite in the high jinxing dance you see on a summer's afternoon, more in a sort of dreamy waltz. A blackbird watched over her shoulder, not much affected. Then he was back on his beaten track: round the house, along the terrace, a quick dash under the mahonia and under the double gates into the field. (The very particular civility in the matter of gates on the part of fellow creatures here is that the fence has rabbit mesh round it: gates provide a squeeze-under which saves the effort of a 3 foot vertical climb and descent when small things are in no hurry.)

When I drove back from taking the post the sparrowhawk on the wire didn't bother to move, and the hare by the gate only loped a car's length away then stood watching me, his black-tipped ears seeming to double his height.

The strangeness out there was that the silence was, quite suddenly, overflowing with birdsong.

The radio said that London had had its highest February temperature since, since ... records began. I put the central heating off. I lay watching twilight greys take possession of the winter sky and a pipistrelle dashed past the window, and another. Not so foolish: I'd wafted my hand through gathering midges as I opened the gate.

And of course geese are supposed to start laying on Valentine's day.

MARCH

March winds. *In like a lion, out like a lamb* – though you'd think vice versa the likelier, with a chance of equinoctial gales. Yet wind is not what strikes me about this month: of all the high winds I've recorded over the years, not one has been in March. January's the windiest month here; December, a not-too-close second. The gale I remember most vividly was on New Year's Eve, gusts so strong we moved furniture away from the window and spread dust sheets ready to catch shards if the six foot wide sheet of plate glass shattered. It flexed with every blast, candle reflections (overhead power lines were down) lurching wildly.

The greatest inconvenience a wind can do is to lift bodily the pair of five-bar gates at the entrance and jam them backwards on to the track, so that it takes crowbars and wedges and levers to free yourself from imprisonment. But the most damage a wind can do is in early summer, when trees are heavy with sap and new growth. Twenty-year old ash trees in particular seem to suffer then, huge branches snapping down – one of the old names for ash is 'widow-maker'. So maybe it's just a characteristic of ash trees, I tell myself, when a young tree looks horribly deformed by the loss of its leader. I know now that, a couple of years on, it will have re-built itself, maybe not so straight but just as strongly. A birch will even re-build itself straight and throw up a new leader.

Clear skies make for contrary days: brilliant sunshine that draws you outdoors, but air that holds its chill in the shade, the moors still shiny under ice and the mountain white-capped. It's too sunny for a coat. Then I'm cold. I'm indoors, then out again like a yo-yo.

In March, everything's on the move, especially daylight as the solstice approaches. The tawny owl swoops out of a cypress tree in the garden five minutes later each day. One or two young trees (birch, rowan) will show precocious leaves by the middle of the month, though for the most part trees merely take on the coloured haze of their bud cases - smoky purple around the alders, dark red around the birches.

March is when you're always noticing the *first* of something: first buds, first oyster catchers, first primroses, first goose eggs, first frogspawn – even the first curlew in years when they're late. You're unlikely to be able to spot the first hazel flowers as it seems to hedge its bets over many months: even in late summer, you can find nascent tight green catkins sheltering underneath the leaves. They've been out dangling in the breeze on one bush or another for a few weeks now. Already some are dried and stiff, some are still green, others long and pale yellow, pollen blowing freely from the leafless twigs. For years I've wondered whether bushes in the shade have longer catkins than those in sun. Having been out with a tape measure today, I cast doubt on my own theory. But some bushes do have much longer catkins than others; if a bush has a record-breaker, all its catkins are long ones. Today's record is five inches.

I was also out with a magnifying glass, because the female flowers are tiny and disregarded. On top of an ordinary-looking bud-like structure is a cluster of lipstick-pink-red fronds, like an arboreal sea-anemone. In spite of their vivid colour, they're so tiny they're easy to miss. The male and female flowers on any one bush don't seem to peak at the same time, which must favour cross-pollination.

The first frogspawn's worth spotting as it forewarns you the great frog-orgy's not far off. Frogs 'know', they say, when the weather has eased enough not to freeze their ponds. I've never seen frogspawn iced over at any rate. The timing varies. As I write, it's the middle of the month, and at some distance from the pond you can hear them chirping: sounds like droplets falling into empty metal pails, as well as a throaty rasp. Your movement or your shadow will make the pond motionless but if you keep still, within seconds bundles of legs and bodies resume their wrestling all over the surface. What you thought was a dead leaf on the bottom mud kicks out to join in. Already there's a huge raft of spawn two metres wide attached to the iris roots at the north side of the pond. Miss today's activity, and you'll have to wait another year: tomorrow there'll only be a few small latecomers swimming around.

At the month end in 2000, alongside the frogspawn was what looked at first to be grass turned glutinous underwater: I scratched away a little of its surface slime, and realised it was a long ribbon of toad spawn with tiny dots, close and random seeming. The first time toads had strung it around this pond.

This year, there's a greater than usual amount of 'failures' – or that's what I used to think of the spoonfuls of caviar and piles of white jelly on the banks of the pond and down the field. Most of them are at one end of the pond – where the water's shallow and there's no step down from the bank – or on a track in that direction from the Old Wood. But as well as failed spawn there's tell-tale lime spattered around: herons have been gobbling the frogs on their way to the pond. (Maybe all the pond weeds make fishing more difficult in the water itself.) It looks as though every other frog part has gone down herons' gullets, so why not the eggs? Since it's only when an egg is actually in the water that its gelatinous covering absorbs water and swells into the familiar black-speck-in-jelly, I assume that herons would become severely dehydrated if they ate the uninflated eggs. But how do they get them *out* of the frogs? Squeeze them before eating?

The first lamb doesn't offer the excitement it once did, as early lambs are often born indoors these days and you only see them outside when they're already strong on their feet. A couple of years back, I saw some day-old blackface lambs all of whom appeared to have been born in a little plastic mac with their head and feet sticking out. Discarded plastic macs littered hedgerows and woodland. No matter, I was told, if you could keep coats dry for the first 48 hours far fewer would become waterlogged in the wet and perish.

The faintest of calls can be enough – I think ears get attuned to particular things – but it took a long time to scry it in 2010, a skein of geese so high it was a mere pencil line sketched on the blue, too high to see individual birds and make any sort of count. It was a long V; there could have been up to three hundred birds heading west for the coast. Most years, pairs of greylags will stop off here for a rest on their voyage, maybe because they see our flock grazing. They circle two or three times, lower and lower, loud wingbeats, before landing. Our birds don't welcome strangers, so the greylags tag along at the edge of the flock, edgy when they see us greeted by our own birds. They're streamlined and slender, feathers in perfect condition. Our hearthed birds have more fat on them and have a side-to-side sway on them when they walk. All right – *waddle*.

But the first goose egg retains all the old magic. You find it by signs: disturbed dry leaves and grass, a few twigs in a circle. Tradition has it geese lay their first egg on St. Valentine's Day: here, it's 6th or 7th March. The dates are so regular, it must mean light plays a greater part in the onset of lay than temperature.

One year, the river was so high in mid-March, the cobble beach was covered by racing brown water, though the grassy banks were still clear. I kept finding goose eggs down there – at least their shells, emptied by predators. I floated them away on the river. The shell of a goose egg is not only larger, but also thicker than a hen's. (I've had some weigh over 500g; 300's more usual.) It has a pointed end of course, as geese are ground-nesting birds and pointed eggs roll in a circle and stay put. It's a structure which is surprisingly difficult to break, even after a growing embryo has absorbed much of the calcium from the shell's granular inner layer. (The largest and strongest structure you can make from any given amount of material is said to be a hollow sphere.) Difficult to break from the outside, that is: the merest tap from the inside by a hatching gosling is enough to make an air-hole, before the gosling wriggles round tapping, rimes the end off its shell and pushes out.

It was the river's March spate that enabled me to get very close to a deer – a roe buck. I'd walked down to the river, the steep way next to the landslip. Between the two woodpiles was a stag, a big fellow, very dark, a six-pointer with velvet on his antlers. He didn't hear my steps, perhaps for the river perpetually rushing; he didn't smell me perhaps for the wild garlic reeking its tender new shoots from wet earth. He looked at me from time to time but I stood tree-still, and he strolled closer and closer – the closest I have ever been to a deer. Such great gobfuls of new growth he wrenched up from the beach, no wonder nothing grows unless guarded. Not a pretty face, short and fat, hamster-like. I was in dark clothes, but my pale face began to puzzle him: he looked me in the eye a long time and then thought just to be on the safe-side he'd bound upwards a little, but nonchalantly as if to show that he wasn't really afraid of a mere tree/person. Oh, the relief to move *my* legs: and when I did, the whole woodland above me exploded in a scattering of hinds, white targets shooting off in all directions.

On 25th March 2000, I resolved to list the wildflowers in the Old Wood throughout the year. I started with primrose, wild strawberry, dog mercury, alchemilla, celandine, wood anemone. I didn't keep it up; there's always too much to do. On the debit side, here are the first nettle shoots, always more, and always in more places. And more than any flock of butterflies could ever need. Then there's creeping thistle to attend to, rushes to cut in the meadow as soon as the land's dry enough for the tractor again...

APRIL

April showers. Stepping out into the first of them, I remember how summer rain smells different from winter rain. It can't do of course: water's just water. It must be grasses and trees breathing out into the wet air that I can smell. And between showers, blue skies, clear air, sharp distances. At the beginning of the month, winter and spring stand alongside: blackthorn's covered in its creamy blossom; further along the same hedgerow, beech holds on to last year's dry pale leaves. (It will keep them until a few days before its long buds are due to unscroll, when there's spring's own leaf-fall.) Avian territories are being settled: a couple of *hoohoo hoohoooo*s from the owl in the cypress tree, a raven seen off by crows, a buzzard bombing an indignant jay, as well as all the smaller song contests.

Mid-month, I see a couple of treecreepers working up the birch trunk by the kitchen window. I've not seen them all winter – where have they been? Down in the woods along the river? They remind me there are many local migrations in addition to the spectacular one of 22nd April (here) when the swallows return. Curlews, oyster catchers and lapwings are already settled back into the valley. A song thrush has returned to the garden; a pied wagtail's flicking along the barn roof. When did we stop hearing the cuckoo in the valley, about 1990?

Male catkins on the goat willow timed themselves perfectly this year to be the palm for Palm Sunday, lit like little lightbulbs by low evening sun against the valley's dark backdrop. Larch cones-to-be look as if they're made of wax, dark red and tiny. Leave home for a couple of days at this time, and you come back to a different world: the possibility of green has become a bright chlorophyll fuzz in the hawthorn. Little yellow-green leaves show the shape of the birch tops in the woods on the opposite side of the valley. Looking from there across to this side, the woods here must have long drifts of white blossom, I planted so many wild cherries. The gean seems to hedge its bets: the first of them was scattering petals at the beginning of the month. Three weeks later, others still keep their buds in tight fists. Whenever a late frost strikes, some will escape.

It's not all primroses, swallows, first purple orchid of the year, special sunsets, chancy encounters with creatures. Two geese – one of which was old and experienced – were sitting on nests near the gate to the bottom meadow three feet apart - just well enough spaced for them not to get mixed up and fight, but close enough for their gander to guard both at once. They were into their third week of sitting when I found torn heaps of down and grass and broken shells and blood and yolk. The mob of crows? The stoat?

Or a bird of prey? A goose crying sounds the same as a human being crying.

I'm inclined to blame the crows. Their raggy black shapes have been flapping around that gateway quite a lot. And I should shoot them. Think *gun* though, and they've vanished. Same with the magpies. There are too many; the population's getting out of control and they're forming a rapacious mob. It's a measurable warfare, about restoring the balance.

Nettles are a different matter. There are so many now – and across footpaths as well – great dark green swathes of them. Yes, they're good for butterflies; but I could feed the whole county's butterflies. All very well allowing nettles their place in a mixed flora, but they have ideas of their own, and not about mixing. They're always dense, never eaten off, so that nothing else can live within or under them; they're a marching monoculture, running their roots under everything else and keeping the light from smaller plants. Come first frost, nettle tops perish and leave – bare earth.

Cutting doesn't control them, seems to provoke them to spread their shoots wider. So I've turned to spraying individual shoots to check the spread of most of these clumps. It takes hours. The leaves blacken and curl – but then where do they and the choking liquid they absorbed go to? I remember DDT.

*

Suppers get later as the evenings grow lighter. I can forget what I'm cooking watching the fells turn pink as the sun sets. I spend a lot of time looking out of the window. One window comes down to the ground. Looking from there one evening, a small movement at my feet made me glance down – a stoat on the step was peering in as intently as I was gazing out. It was the closest I'd been to a stoat: two inches away if you discount the sheet of plate glass. I was surprised by how silky he looked, how long the hairs in the black tip to his tail. And so mischievous a face.

I watched four leverets running about on the hill. They were in the same place in the evening sun the day before, and again in the morning, running – then still when I caught them through binoculars almost as if they felt my gaze. I looked it up: *litter size – four; February to October*. The week before, an adult hare was killed on the road.

A couple of days later, the leverets were replaced on the hill by two stags going through aggressive posing: pawing the ground with a front hoof, head down, then charging at each other. The smaller of the two was bound to lose out, approaching from downhill, but he managed a few charges of his own. He stood up on his hind legs to stop a couple of charges from the larger animal. They were careful to keep at least 20 yards between them – *typical male behaviour*, said Mike. In the evening, a female took the same route over the hill, stopping every now and then to look around.

*

The thick stone slabs that roof this building settle and sag over the years. Only when I look at an old photograph showing a level roof, do I realise how uneven it is now. So much so that the idea takes root that several birds must be nesting in the roof, some at one end (where they sound as if they're inside a cupboard, they're so loud) and some at the other, where the barn's open to its purlins and seems to magnify the sound so that I hear birds with elephants' feet.

Probably starlings, I think to myself, and rush outside when I hear the noises and the faint cheeping sounds of young being fed, expecting to see a bird fly out for more worms. I've not seen one emerge, even when I've left the door open so that I can be sure the noisy activity's stopped. No bird lime marks a threshold anywhere.

Good Friday, the noises are louder than ever: the bird doesn't seem to deliver a couple of worms and depart, quickly and regularly like the blue tits in their orderly box by the gate, but seems to have made a nest where it has to work its way deep into the roof cavity. I thought it would have annoyed me more than it does, but I hear it only two or three times a day. Today the noises continue for three or four minutes: the cries of the young not silenced by filled beaks like they usually are. I run out in the bitter north-easterly and watch the roof. Still no bird. I've left the door wide so I can hear. The noises continue. Then: silence. No bird. I wait. Perhaps it sees me, and waits for me to leave before emerging? I scan every dark cranny across the roof for movement. Nothing. No sound. I'm too chilled to wait any longer. A last glance up the roof before I come in: black eyes peer over the gutter. The stoat.

She floats up, over the ridge and... where? down the other side of the roof? I look all round the building: no movement anywhere, no tell-tale excitement among small birds to signal her whereabouts. Is she raiding the nests in the air like she'll raid goose nests on the ground? Or is it she who lives in the roof? Her young who cry? And how on earth does she get up there?

MAY

May flowers. Gean petals blowing along the track. Brassy patches of gorse. Horse chestnuts out-classing everything for a couple of days before sinking back into their heavy green. The quieter tree flowers show now too, like the knobbly hanging clusters on the oak. No wonder ash is more reticent about leaves: its black buds swell into tiny red and gold flowers then throw up fountains of seeds. Elms – where they still stand – are well on with their seeds already, twigs massing lime green platelets bright as any flowers. My car changes colour in May, covered by an even dusting of pale yellow talcum – birch pollen.

For years I've been meaning to cross to the other side of the valley and look back at the woods I planted on this. All my views are of the woodland opposite (which faces north) and which has only one wild cherry, bright amongst the darker alder and ash. I wonder what this side looks like now all the solid forms of old elms have gone, and now I've planted so many wild cherries.

Tiny and tender new leaves are as bright as flowers themselves, the sun shining through. It's not surprising they've been used for salads: you can't help but think they look appetising. Just-unfurled beech leaves look so fine and delicate you think they'd be nothing on the tongue, but there's already a hint of their fibrous structure. They taste... *green*. And slightly sweet. I've not tried bread-and-cheese, the young leaves on hawthorn. Nor will I bring any of the blossom indoors, lovely though it is with its clean whites fading to pink. *Unlucky indoors* is a last, lingering superstition left from when may was revered for its supernatural powers. Even now, it seems symbolise the burst of growth that happens in the shift from spring to summer.

The *may* may be out in May further south, though here it can be June before the local hedgerows perform. In one rough field here, feathery wild carrot used to flower a white covering all over the ground at the same time as the quickthorn was white with blossom. 'Used to' because badgers discovered them a couple of years ago, grubbing up the pignuts and leaving the field ploughed. I've not tried those either. Ken says they used to dig pignuts and eat them when they were kids.

Primroses are still out at the beginning of the month, in the Old Wood and at the foot of old hedgerows, so thick you can't stop yourself 'Come and see, come and see' – though they look nothing on photographs among last year's brown leaves and mud. But really this is bluebell time in the Old Wood, that blue of distances always deeper in. Wild garlic crowds the lower slopes. One wood alongside the road to the village fills your car with lasting garlic reek every time you drive by.

I know, now, to look for the small overlooked things: owl pellets under the old ash, crammed with tiny bones; hazelnut shells on the ground, with one neat hole but all of them left whole side up, or insignificant flowers. One tiny flower I didn't know, neither yellow nor green, appeared like small lamps, among the grass. Their scent was strong, sweet but serious. You could feel the thin stem was four-sided. My old Keble-Martin was the only book clear enough to identify the elegant architecture at the end of this flower stem, five-petalled flowers facing NSE and W like a clock tower, and one at the top with only four petals facing the sky. I should say, heaven – Keble-Martin adds a completely uncharacteristic aside to his formal classification: *a symbol of Christian watchfulness.* Since then, I've found moschatel on the banks of shady lanes and by streams, in quite big patches: becoming, like everything else, much easier to see when you have a name for it.

Everyone, even those who've never heard one before, would know if they heard a cuckoo who *sings his song in May.* There's a red ring on the calendar around 5th May 2010: I heard a cuckoo calling first thing in the morning. It's the cause of much excitement and conversation. Norman, dropping the milk bottles into the rack, said it arrived on Saturday, didn't I hear it, going at it on Perry Moor all day Sunday? He reckons it must be seven or eight years since we heard the last one. I say the way time goes, more like ten. You can soon get fed up with it though, *cuckoo cuckoo cuckoo* as monotonous and aggravating as... well, as a cuckoo clock gone wrong. Except that in the still of the evening, when it moved from the moor to the valley, close by at the top of the Old Wood, the sound was as rich as a woodwind, almost breathy.

Has it moved on? Calls, but no response from a female.

Winter-flowering heather by the garden gate has been out for weeks now, a pinky-mauve mat that you smell and hear before you're upon it. You can smell its dark honey, but these days it's silent: even on the sunniest days there are no honey bees. Bumble bees crawled over it drunkenly in early sunshine, and there are a few small furry red bees (another order of life I don't know enough about to name) and flies, but no honey bees. I've read about 'colony collapse disorder' as it's called in the States, but that name's just descriptive. Bee damage seems complex. A parasitic mite has infested hives, taking with it bee viruses and bee diseases. But mites and viruses have always been around and amateur bee keepers' hives seem healthier than commercial ones. Feeding commercial bees on industrial sugars may not have been the best nutrition for their well-being and resilience. The British Bee Keeping Association suggests we underplant nursery and horticultural crops with clover to provide more high quality nectar for bees. Manufacturers of newer systemic chemical crop treatments claim these are no more damaging to bee life than foliar sprays applied externally at times when bees are not foraging. Yet the change in spraying is coincident with sick hives, so you wonder. (And recently, so does the E.U.)

Meanwhile, I'll go with the mobile phone theory. Looking against the light when the sun is low in the evenings, you can see the air is a thick soup of tiny flying creatures and dust and pollen and seed and gossamer. There's no 'empty' air any signals can pass though. Do signals upset wind-borne pollens and seed distribution as well as bees?

The apples flower throughout May, the earliest in the first week or so, along with the crabapples as an extra pollinator. No bees in their pink and white cupped flowers either. The plums flowered at the end of last month, but I can't tell yet whether the soggy brown remnants of their blooms have actually *set*. I think the small green nubs at the centres *will* be fruit, but that may be wishful thinking.

We think of summer as the dry season. Dry weather jobs include carting poles and tree trunks from the Old Wood: it takes weeks of sunny weather before you're able to drive a tractor across the bottom field and into the wood without making deep ruts or getting stuck. But the elm felled three years ago and stacked wigwam has been inaccessible for the last two summers. Spring seems to be the dry season these days. So we're leaving grass uncut and fetching logs instead, hauling heavy weights over ground baked so hard we leave no wheel tracks.

I'm buying-in logs to season over the summer from the woodyard above the village as well, extras to keep in store for 'emergencies' – a long winter, an extra cold one, or visitors who need to be warmer. Dick brought a load of sycamore and beech yesterday, gloomy about supplies, what with farms using fallen trees for biofuel, that biomass plant in Dumfries gobbling up millions of tons of good hardwoods that should have gone for logs and timber, even Lambert's running short, let alone all the folk who fitted wood-burners when coal got pricey. By the time he leaves, I'm worrying about tree poaching taking over from sheep rustling and imagining a treeless landscape. And pay up gratefully.

*

On May Day 1997 there were half a dozen mallard chicks on the pond, and a moorhen scooting out of sight. There should be goslings following their parents round the fields by now, but over the last few years the flock has lost more and more geese to badgers. A sitting goose is such an easy meal for a badger – she won't fly, but will try to defend her eggs. Or goslings. This isn't good land for badgers: the soil's too wet and too heavy and too shallow for setts. They must be extending their night-time foraging as their numbers increase. And that also explains the absence of curlew nests in the meadow, and oyster catcher nests down on the river's cobble beach. These would be even safer nesting sites as far as human activity goes than they were a few years ago, when sitting curlews were something I expected to come across in the hay, and oyster catchers screamed at you and distracted you if you went down to the river. (Though if you sit completely still for a time, they'll forget you and return to their eggs.)

I've spent long twilights sitting out down the field, trying to forestall attack. It's futile, but when nests are destroyed and geese ripped apart you can't *not* try. There are still a few birds calling at first, and you can easily be startled when pheasants hurtle from their roost in a tree as you walk underneath. Colours fade down to greys, but the night seems never quite to arrive because eyes gradually adjust – though as time passes, you realise you're relying more and more on your ears to know what's going on, straining for the crack of twigs, rustle of grass as a creature passes. (No need to listen hard for deer in the Old Wood – two roe bucks in a barking competition.) You even pick up the sound of an aeroplane way overhead, usually too high to be heard. Bats circle and jink. Back home, you'll find your wrist between glove and coat braceleted with midge bites.

Dew falls, and draws out scents of dampness, sweetness, promise.

At the month end, small birds are feeding their young, cherries and gooseberries are already the size of peas. The first roses have opened. And still the ash trees hold back. *We'll only have a splash.*

JUNE

Flaming June. And the sun *is* hotter out of a clear sky, making leafy shade feel like a different world, cooler and with an evening drift of scent from the last azalea blossoms. The stone building, roofed with stone slabs, stays cool. This year, the month does flame, with temperatures of 28 even up here in the hills where there's still a breeze. Humidity's high too – between 80% and 90%, everything growing at once, all the roses rushing into bloom and over, a row of rocket living up to its name and finished 3 weeks after seeds were planted. But the temperature also hurries the strawberries along. They're ahead of the raspberries and gooseberries this year. Every evening, another bowlful. So many, they have to be given away.

Of course if the weather's cold, there's an equally appropriate saying: *Cowquake June* – an expectation of things even-ing themselves out, if there's been a *Blackthorn winter*. Do things even themselves out? Ken reports his father insisted grass grows the same amount every year – just does it at different times. A dry and cold spring means it's not grown at all this year: most people are short of grazing. No one's cut silage yet.

The leaf canopy in the woods has thickened, and the flush of flowers across the woodland floor is done. Trees have taken on their solid summer shapes, eating away sections of the long distance views. No, not all the trees: a cherry and a small leaf lime near the house have died: they've struggled for years in poor and waterlogged soil. And the alders – so many have failed. The chain of young trees along the river bank is leafless.

I'd always assumed 'somebody' had planted the old alders on the opposite side of the river, roots interlaced like knobbly arthritic fingers to hold the bank in place. Then ten years ago the river shifted its channel adding a few yards of levelled rock and soil on this side, at the bottom of the Old Wood. Alders appeared forthwith, a thick band of seedlings at the water's edge. Their cones must have stranded among rocks when the river was in flood. They grew quickly, able to fix nitrogen with their roots: already their trunks are wider than I can span with both hands.

But this year, no leaves. We shall lose them all, and maybe even the old alder up by the house which two people couldn't even span with both arms. It's death by a fungus disease that invades the roots and makes lesions which kill the trees. Alder's always seemed robust, but in the last few years a new phytophthora has developed, a cross between the fungus that attacks beech roots and strawberry blight, and it is *spreading across Europe as a 'hybrid swarm' which consists of multiple forms of the pathogen. Some of the variants are very damaging and pose a serious threat to alder and the stability of riparian ecosystems.* You can frighten yourself reading government forestry reports like this.

This *hybrid swarm* is my third disaster. The first happened the day I bought the Old Wood. Quarter of an acre of it slipped away downriver, which felt like a very bad omen. The mud and rock have more-or-less grown over now. (Other landslides have happened since: birch – and alder – quickly colonise bare soil.) The second disaster was Dutch elm disease, whose beetle vector worked its way steadily upstream along the Old Wood over the next three years. But looking across at the woodland on the opposite side of the valley, I don't see any holes in the canopy. I have to think about it to remember those clear yellow cumulus shapes now missing from the autumn colours.

We felled most of the dead elms on the steep slopes to stop them falling, tearing out their rootballs and causing more landslides. One of them has thrown up from its base a strong new shoot the deer missed because of a bramble, its bark not yet thick enough for beetles, but still too young to flower. If it can flower and fruit before the beetles bore in…

One old elm at the top of the wood, a little away from the others, escaped. In 2007, I could see a couple of small patches of dead wood way up in its top branches. *You're the boss*, Ken said ominously when I asked him to drop it, *but it's still alive, hardly any disease only that bit at the top, seems a shame.* The argument in favour of felling, that its root system was still strong, sounded a bit thin. But when we looked at the tree, we could see where it had been felled many times before: it had seven thick trunks and we'd only be doing what used to be done. These old elms had been part of a rotation coppice for the bobbin mill downriver. Maybe it wasn't that much of a risk after all. *Which way do you want it dropped?*

We stacked the felled trunks. Fetched fence posts and American netting and rabbit mesh and built a high defensive compound round the stump – though we never imagined there'd be such a dense burgeoning of leaf and shoot sprouting out as there was in the spring. Does it need thinning? No one remembers the last time the Old Wood was worked: there's no one alive to ask.

My idea of disasters is changing. They depend on your time-scale.

I shall need to remember this when the next disaster arrives. About half the trees in the woodlands here are ash, most grown from local seed, although a few were bought from a nearby nursery in the early 1990s – I was too young then to have overwintered seed, set out seedlings in a nursery and wait a year… a year seemed such a long time. And now I'm thinking in decades. It could take that long for the ash here to be affected by *Chalara fraxinea*. There's time to plan ahead. I need to start growing seedlings in the gaps to take over from ash. But what is an alternative? What is fast, vigorous, strong, useful and bears sprays of black and-gold flowers on bare twigs in March? I want ash to survive. I'll collect seed from healthy stock each year and store it in the fridge, and replenish it each year if the stock is still healthy. I'll be agitating for tree movements to cease; nobody's going to want to plant ash anyway now. Wind-borne fungal spores don't generally travel great distances, but lorries do – and fungus spores travel happily in the soils and composts we move around by road.

*

The goose pasture is covered with worn out and faded feathers from the adult birds' moult, grounding them for a week or so. (They'll grow smart new wing feathers the colour of milky coffee about the same time as goslings become fully feathered.) By the middle of the month, most young birds are ready to fly. There was a great commotion in the close-packed leaves of the beech hedge this morning, and a young song thrush wobbled out from the nest to its first view of the world beyond the leaves. It still had the wide, bright yellow banding round its beak, and it stood optimistically giving a rather bewildered-looking squawk for more food. And then: its first flight: down on to the grass at the edge of a flower bed. All of ten yards, with the wings (I almost said leaves) whirring frantically. No tail yet; a round, ungainly thing on far-too long legs as it hopped sensibly into the cover of the flowerbed.

It looked larger than the mother bird who has carried so much food into the nest this past few weeks, thin and bedraggled in the rain. I say 'mother' for the male of the pair is an extraordinarily aggressive bird, who has spent his parenthood singing territorial songs from the electricity pole. His voice is loud. His song repertoire is extensive, and now includes curlew calls – so realistically that I look up to see them passing. He can also do telephone rings. My answering-machine cuts in after four rings: he's learned a four-ring call, as well as a Calor Gas wagon reversing.

The bird box I see from the kitchen window is a prime nesting site: there are always arguments about which pair is going to take vacant possession each spring. The parent bluetits look worn and tattered by the time their offspring leave for the beech hedge below, especially the female, who flew in about 400 loads of moss and twig for the nest, before lining it with her own breast down and sitting on the eggs and then supplied the young with their 10500 larvae – I can't remember where I read these figures, but they're unforgettable.

Not much writing gets done in June. It's a month when you're needed outdoors – if it's fine, there's a first cut to the pastures if you're going to keep on top of creeping thistle and dock and nettle, which have surged into strong dark stands by now. Then there's light rain, and the evening air smells so lovely with its drifts of scent, that you hang around the garden, neither writing nor working, or you wander round the fields in the last of the light, looking at how things are growing and trying to remember to put this job or that on the list for another day or another season. You end up watching bubbles rise to the surface on the pond. Bubbles? No, something taking a fly. Four inches of dark something that rises vertically, touches the surface and wiggles straight back down. The light's poor; you can't quite make it out.

If there are fish in the pond, how did they get there? It was built by digging down – about twelve feet deep in the middle – and puddling the clay fifteen years ago. It fills from land drains running down from the fields above. For years it was only water, mud and methane until in desperation I sank a pot of Canadian pond weed in the middle. The water cleared. A ring of burr reed appeared where the water's about two feet deep. That's explicable: birds could have dropped the seed. Frogs, toads, newts – they're all explicable, too. Fish?

Could be eels, thinks Ken, and tells me about cleaning out a water trough once and seeing a foot-long eel wriggle out of the pipe from the spring that fed it, across the bottom of the trough and away down the drain pipe. I think what I've got looked fatter than eels. It'll need a few more evenings down at the pond to sort this one.

JULY

My parents married on 15th July. It was always easy to remember their anniversary, St. Swithun's day. Or was it the other way round – easy to remember St. Swithun's day because it was their anniversary? *If it rains on St. Swithun's*, my mother would start saying at the beginning of the month, *it'll rain forty days and forty nights*. (This year, it's rained enough in the first week to make up for that hot dry June: a stone trough which depends on rainwater has gone from dry to full in three days.)

I've always thought of Swithun as a sort of patron saint of heavy rain – but that's because my mother seemed to know only the rainy part of the rhyme which goes on, I've recently discovered, to predict a sunny 15th will likewise ensure forty good days and nights. Not that Swithun had anything to do with either rainmaking or sunbathing. It's just that his name-day was as useful for thinking about weather patterns for haymaking as it is for remembering to buy anniversary cards.

These old sayings and weather lore must have provided generalisations about harvesting with better odds than evens. It made me wonder if there's a predictable pattern in the jetstream that governs our weather: if it moves south on or by 15th July, does it stay there? Apparently it does – about the middle of the month the jetstream settles into a groove and the prospects for change are low for a good six weeks. Until St Bartholemew's day. This year, I resolve to count out the forty days.

I always forget, though from notes I know that in 2002 Swithun was benign. The hay had been cut and turned and the house was full of the dry smell of grass and pollen. Seed heads on the long grasses in the Goose Field were mauve and delicious to the meadow browns and tiny moths flitting round you as you walked through. The hay was tossed and spread and spread and spread in a fog of pollens and dust and then – this is what I like best – windrowed in long curving rows of candyfloss the length of the field, the height of the pile a first measure of how thick is the crop. Then the baler thumping and the fields stripped naked.

Sometimes the valley seems to have a weather system all its own. That year, there was a wedding a mile up the valley. There were towering clouds, and you could see heavy showers all round, but the valley had wedding weather: warm sun, not a breath of wind. Then I heard leaves down in the Old Wood rustle, and heard its progress up the field: a whirlwind. It spiralled madly through the still air, across the flower beds and off towards the wedding. I saw one once clothe itself in dust and process slowly down the track towards the river, as if it were following the path along the ground and not through the air.

This month started where the last left off: with small birds. A fledgling flycatcher was standing on the tarmac in the sun a couple of days ago, looking around bewildered at the change of scenery from nest to world. It was in the same spot half an hour later – not good to be so exposed to a passing predator. When I crouched to check whether it was all right, it hopped on to my arm – too young, too innocent to have classed human beings as a threat. I stood with it on my wrist, in close-up, then slowly walked round the house to where I'd seen its parents using the gate as a perch from which they did their fly fishing. A sudden chatter of alarm from a parent, and the little thing whirred off into a bush.

*

In 2002, a questionnaire from the Forestry Commission asked: *Are the Works up-to-date?* I ticked the boxes. *The Works* were then ten years old, ash trees growing exceptionally well. This isn't good soil for cherry wood and I'd planted fewer, but they've done well too, stately and straight enough to make fine tables and cupboards some day. That year I was able to pick a few wild cherries the birds had missed, pale cream flushing pink and then red. I found one tree doing its own thing and growing yellow cherries, which the birds ignored entirely.

Because birds are happy with sour cherries, we rarely find many ripe ones for ourselves. But four years after that first fruiting, every one of the cherry trees was so weighed down by the crop it bore, the birds couldn't keep up. We were able to collect bagsful with ease. Even passing deer grazed on cherries. Geoffrey Grigson says that the wild fruit used to be sold around the streets of London on the branch. I suppose that would keep it fresh – certainly the picked fruits don't last long. But I'm surprised branches were cut; that takes away fruit-bearing wood.

Each tree carries slightly different fruit. Several bear ripe fruit almost black. Most are red-fruited, some with light orangey-red fruits, others with much darker red cherries. I'd guess one in twenty is white- or yellow-fruited. Wild cherries are smaller and sharper than garden cherries, but all the same delicious enough for you to make yourself decidedly unwell, guzzling while picking. Geese will eat every one you drop, stone included, and without ill-effects.

I saw a couple of fledgling blackbirds under a cherry tree out of the wind, wings spread in the warmth, looking up at the ripe fruits, waiting merely for luck to fall, beaks open. Sometime the unplucked fruit must fall. Later I saw one of them with a cherry in its wedged-wide beak – unable to crush it and unwilling to put it down, head to one side then the other, not knowing quite what to do with the bright gleam of its desire.

*

No milk for me, thank you. He pulls the chair away from the table and settles in: *I'll just take the weight off while it cools.* This is going to be a long session. The first rain after a dry month, but still there's nothing moving: worms must be dropping straight into the runs. He's been mole-catching (a pause while he calculates) just over sixty year now. Three thousand a year, that's a lot of moles. (A pause while we calculate.) Yes, a lot of moles and still they tunnel on, undeterred.

In places where there are old, long established runs, they can be left to themselves and their underground lives. It's new workings – maybe at this time of year young moles sculling around just under the surface – that cause trouble, throwing up stones that catch in machinery, or soil into hay that makes it spoil in store before the season is out. Any kindly feelings remaining towards moles from *Wind in the Willows* soon evaporate if you care for a lawn they're intent on undermining. Get one in your vegetable patch, and you'll happily join the pursuit: the only time I've known a mole work in a straight line has been along a row of vegetables. Roots disrupted, your winter crop fails.

Only when moles go deep do they throw up hills. The last few weeks have been dry: worms burrowed deeper into damp earth, and the moles after them – the resulting hills, enormous. There are a couple of astonishing hills among young trees near the house, a foot high and over a yard across. Nests, maybe – though on the whole they nest and overwinter in the cops, the built-up hedgerows that provide havens above the water table even in heavy rain.

Tea without milk takes a long while to cool. We're on to the price of coal now. He can tell me exactly how much I paid for nuggets last time I had them, and that was years ago. Now he's retired, all the time in the world, he does a bit of keepering as well. He's always had all the time in the world: even when he had the coal yard, you'd see him stood motionless in a field, listening for moles. He can't hear them scratting so well these days, he has to wait until they throw some soil up, then he can get them: you don't shoot at the heap, but below that, where they've come from. He digs out the dead, so he can tell you how many he's caught. I've never known him do his accounts by hanging corpses along a fence. (Someone's hung 73 on barbed wire by the moor road. I've just counted.) I suppose he works among friends, and he's trusted.

He'll trap moles as well as shoot them. He told me last year my soil was *too murley for traps*. This time he shows me his traps, rough-carved, thick wooden half-cylinders with bits of string and wire – like nothing I've seen before, and their wood polished with use.

The tea must be cold by the time he says he talks to owls. He likes them. One night he must have had a dozen round him, were they confused! *Here, I'll show you.* He feels in a pocket: binder twine, bits of paper, fencing staples – and a spent cartridge. He squeezes the end, slots it between his fingers and curls his fist, then blows gently over his knuckles. A tawny owl calls softly from the beam above our heads; another answers from its territory in the rafters of the main room.

I'll leave it with you he says, putting the yellow cartridge into my hand when he goes.

No amount of blowing on my part has produced the faintest of hoots. Well, he did smile when he gave it me.

AUGUST

Not much *glorious* about this 12th as I write: heavy cloud, a cold airstream from the north and high humidity – not that there'd be shooting on the moor today anyway: it's a Wednesday.

Burnmoor's four miles away, our skyline from the kitchen window. When Open Access Land was proposed, this piece of high moorland was listed as having been in continuous exclusive private use longer than any other land in England. So the day the Countryside and Rights of Way Act 2000 came into force, we walked it – wondering whether owners of such land all over the country were nervously watching out for coachloads of rampant walkers. There was no one on the hill but us, no one but us amazed by the long distance views of Peaks, Lakes and Irish Sea opening up all round as we climbed.

We often walk there now: so close to home, and yet in no time we can be out on wild moorland. At the top (or nearly so – the trig point's a hundred yards further on) is The Standard Stone. It's a large squarish block with STANDARD elegantly carved corner-to-corner across its top surface. It's well-weathered but I've found no one yet who can tell me when it was put there. On the map, it's marked as 'Standard on Burn Moor' and you can see it's a boundary stone for Lancashire / Yorkshire. Three sides are lettered: T, B, N. It took us several visits to realise that when you stand at the stone to read N, you're facing north. T and B must stand for the parishes that lie to its west and east.

In all the times we've been up there, we've only met one other person (holidaying in B) and he was lost. We are, after all, animals. Like all animals we have our habits: we stick to our tracks and paths. We don't go wandering all over Open Access Land, but assiduously follow guidebooks and marked paths. On Burnmoor we tramp along a quad bike's tyre tracks: off-piste it would be hard work, wading through clumps and dips in the heather.

What would the hill be without its heather? Cotton grass, moss, bog? For years we've taken for granted that Burnmoor's a heather-covered hill, purpling briefly towards the end of this month, but this is a high-maintenance landscape, sectioned and burned off, so some of the heather's always regenerating. The grouse population is wild and sustained only by heather's young shoots.

And so is another creature: heather beetle. I hear it's suddenly rife after several mild winters and wet summers, giving rise to anxiety about the survival of those grouse which survive the guns. It's an extraordinary practice, a whole landscape and its populations managed for a few people to spend a day or two taking shots at birds whirring and dipping low over the ground, and equally extraordinary that a mere beetle can munch that practice to pieces. Over time, I suppose the beetle population would fall: more and more of their parasitoid wasps would lay eggs into the beetle grubs and have their own brief heyday in turn, and then grouse numbers would improve again. But such natural cycles don't respect the annual shooting parties we've legislated for.

August races towards autumn. The first sign is berries – already ripe on the rowans. (I used to think rowan berries were orange. Some are, but each tree's different: those with yellowy-orange berries have yellowy-green leaves, whereas the leaves on those with deep crimson berries are a deep blue-ish green.) Darkness is on the move – the long northern twilights no longer make a bid for the small hours. Sometimes now it's dark when we get home. If we drive back in rain after a sunny day that's warmed the tarmac, our track can be impassable: hundreds of toads sit there, rain-bathing. This appears to be a blissful activity: car, headlights, horn, shouts – nothing disturbs them. They don't swell and put their heads down in their 'defence position' but sit there, you could imagine, smiling. You have to get out and put them in the long grass either side of the track – which can make for a very slow 200 yards if you're on your own, or have a squeamish passenger. A toad's defensive skin secretions are known to make dogs very sick, but so far I'm OK.

I watched the daylight fading last night and the bats hurtling round the garden. I can never tell whether it's ten different bats I see or the same bat ten times on the same circuit. Between bats, an owl flew up to the roof – one who knew what he was about, since he went straight to the chimney and used the stove and its pipe as a sounding box. A second one glided up to join him – maybe this was the pair which has overwintered in the cypress tree near the house the last two years, checking us out again now nesting is over.

After breeding comes this stake-out of winter territories. Lots of creatures are on the move. Eighteen years ago today (old notebooks always amaze) I glanced up from reading a Sunday paper and saw a roe deer by the gate, grazing. I'd already photographed one just there, and since the sound of a shutter alarms them as much as would a shot, I continued to read. Later she – or perhaps another – was there again. The wind was westerly, lifting my scent and small sounds away from her as I walked slowly out towards her, more or less obscured by the hedge. I held still each time she lifted her head checking routinely all round. A wren chittered at length, but the deer paid less attention to the warning than I did behind the gatepost, trying to blend with its shape and so close that I heard the tearing sound as she pulled at the grasses. A small movement to my left: her kid was with her. It was a lighter softer shade of gold: the mother was almost as dark and as red as a red deer would be. The small creature's legs were as thin as a greyhound's. It left most of the scanning to its mother as they took a step, fed, took another step another mouthful but once it raised its head and swivelled its radar ears right round: thick dark eyelashes above large eyes, and a very black muzzle – all the features Lorenz says will tug at a human heart.

That old notebook also quotes Barry Lopez: *Few things provoke like the presence of wild animals. They pull at us like tidal currents.* He was writing about encounters with lone animals while out in the Arctic. We can often meet a deer, or some other creature, at close quarters and usually they don't flee but stand waiting for us to leave. But if we're alone, and the animal is too, the look we exchange feels more penetrating, one species considering another. Such encounters leave me wondering about their *wildness.* They seem so – *anachronistic* is almost the right word – *out of their element* in this landscape, every hectare of which is managed, mowed, planted, fenced, contained. Yet here they are, casually strolling through this manned place, as if they've just come from somewhere else. Except there isn't anywhere else for them to be at home in.

*

August traditionally shakes off St Swithun's forty days of weather on St Bartholomew's day. There's been some sun from time to time, but here in the north west the forty days have been cool and often wet. On day 38, avoiding Burnmoor and its shooting parties, we walked along the edge of another high moor land, Goober Common – no heather here: rough grassland, cotton grass and rushes, wintering grounds for lapwings and ringed plovers. It had been breezy with broken cloud when we set out, but we were caught by three thunder / hail storms – and there's no shelter on open moorland. Anywhere further from home and we'd have walked equipped for changing weather.

Twenty-fourth fair and clear, a prosperous autumn follows this year.

SEPTEMBER

A sting on my left hand, stained fingers, scratched arms, nettled ankles – blackberry time again. *Even fools grow fat in September.* You can put off planting in the spring by a couple of days if need be, but harvesting has to be done when it has to be done. And so does jam- and chutney-making. In September, I'm sure September's the worst month for writing.

Blackberrying must be done before the devil pisses on the fruits in October, but there no longer seems much competition for my favourite patches: no one's been trampling the hedgerow grasses before me. Jam-making's not the compulsion it used to be for most people, though I've not lost it. My father, at 96, still makes his own and says he's never bought jam or marmalade either and isn't about to start now.

I remember jars of jam and pickle and bigger jars of bottled fruit on high shelves all round a kitchen of a great aunt and uncle in the 1950s. I remember my mother making raspberry jam when I was eleven, remember it not setting, and her tipping the jars back into the pan to boil it up for longer. (My parents moved house so often when I was a child, I can date memories by houses

– the kitchen in which the jam failed to set was wallpapered with bunches of green flowers on a white background. I liked the sprig which I thought of then as cow parsley, but was more likely fennel.) Jam-making / pickling is what you do in September.

2009 was a poor year for apples (after a bumper crop the year before), but a medium one for damsons. The previous year there were none at all, and none in the Lythe Valley either. I've planted some half-standard damson trees, but the tastiest fruit is on a crabbed old hedgerow tree. I've heard this from others round here, too – disappointed with the fruits of a new tree, they end up nurturing root suckers from some ancient, bent tree they'd taken for granted. (An ancient *un*-grafted tree of course.) Fruits are one thing we've not improved on lately. That favourite English plum, Victoria, dates from 1840. The dark purple cooking plum, Czar, was introduced in 1875; the best for jam-making, Pershore (aka Yellow Egg), in 1827.

I've planted several varieties of old apple in the Goose Field, though I'm too far north to have many to choose from. Keswick Coldlin (1793) was an obvious one since it's fairly local, having been found near Ulverston. But it's Early Victoria, a nineteenth-century cross from Keswick Codlin, that has made me realise what we've lost: I have to remember to pick it – this is a cooker that can be ready, in a good year, by the end of July. The English apple season therefore (think how well Bramleys store) can last 9 or 10 months. Early Victoria's a bright, light green that turns yellow when ripe, and it's a strange shape: 'oblong-conical' catalogues call it. It has vertical ribs, some with sharp hair-lines, and flat sides. It wouldn't do at all on a supermarket shelf. Modern breeders looking for new apples want consistent size and shape and heavy crops and rosy skins that will resist being stored and transported. Taste? – for that you need discriminating consumers, like the Victorians with their estates and walled gardens and head gardeners and orchards, or a rural population that works in the countryside and depends on its cottage gardens, rather than supermarkets and East Malling Research.

I planted a Cox of course, but this is too far north for it to thrive and it only produces a few small fruits now and again. An English Cox, allowed to ripen on the tree before being picked, hasn't been bettered. Most of the 'Cox' apples imported from the southern hemisphere are a sport of the original. On the rare occasions I've had 'real' Coxes, it's been in an apple–league of its own. (Sometimes the Wednesday market stall in the village has a box of real Coxes at this time of year; you can tell, the stall-holder's eating them.) Last year Ashmead's Kernel ran it close, though only last year. It's not just the size and quantity of the fruits that change each year, but the flavour, too. *Every year's good for something*, Ken will say whenever I complain about the weather.

Cox's Orange Pippin was raised by Richard Cox, a brewer and gardener in Slough, who used his two acre paddock for his hobby: apples. About 1825, he sowed two seeds from Ribston

Pippin (an apple raised in Yorkshire a century earlier from French seeds collected near Rouen). The two seedlings went out into his garden – and both (having been sold on to nurserymen) were in production by 1840 as Cox's Orange Pippin and Cox's Pomona (a cooking apple). How wonderful to breed a fruit like that. You can read the history of apples in their names, a history of keen gardeners like Cox sowing seeds, or coming across self-sown wildings along the hedgerows. D'Arcy Spice was found in a garden at Tolleshunt d'Arcy in Essex; Duke of Devonshire was raised near here, at Holker Hall, in 1835; Golden Noble was 'discovered' by Patrick Flanaghan, the gardener at Stowe Hall in Norfolk. In apple nomenclature, aristocrats rub shoulders with cottagers. Granny Smith sprang from a chance seed thrown out by a Mrs Thomas Smith in Ryde, New South Wales that had fruited by 1868. (It doesn't 'do' in northern Europe.) Bedfordshire Foundling speaks for itself. And so on. The only one to regret is A.H. Mullins's 1890 find of a chance seedling in Clay County, West Virginia: Golden Delicious.

I continue to spit my pips and stones just in case, though the odds against finding good chance seedlings are much higher these days: we no longer have the same number of varieties around for cross pollination. A small, lumpy bitter green fruit is all I've discovered in a hedgerow here.

*

By mid-month, both ends of the day are changing so fast they always take you by surprise. The evenings are dark now before we've finished eating. Clear nights are cold. This morning the world was as white as if there'd been a heavy frost: it was a dew, droplets on leaves winking prismatic colours in the sun – a dew so heavy it's going to take all day to dry.

When the air's still like this, the valley collects sound from every direction. I'd been hearing a raven on and off all morning (Terry the mole-catcher had told me there were a couple of pairs up on the moor). When I fetched the binoculars, I saw two land on a fence at the top of the hill. A third joined them, *pruuk-pruuk*. A family outing? They gleamed in the sun as if they'd been varnished. They suddenly took off together – to attack a buzzard, who was quickly outmanoeuvred. I'd not realised before how much bigger ravens are than buzzards: binoculars on a single bird don't give you scale.

Ten minutes later, the buzzard settled on the fence where the ravens had been.

Equinoctial gales blasted away the still, dew-soaked mornings on the proper day in 2009, bringing down twigs and quite a few leaves already turned yellow – mainly birch. I suppose it's because part of me is still thinking about sailing that I watch the winds so carefully. I've always assumed that not only were there strong winds at the equinox, but also more of them. Now I look at the records, it's not that there are more gales at the autumn equinox, but that winds increase in frequency from now on, and gradually tail off in March and early April. Some, at least, of our autumn winds are increased by Atlantic depressions absorbing warm air left behind when a hurricane has dissipated after crossing cool waters. There'll be a very high tide down in the town this week, with these onshore westerlies pushing in the equinoctial high spring tides.

The last day of the month, and how odd it feels to be able to pick a small bowl of raspberries. It's the first time I've grown primocanes, which fruit twice, precociously on new shoots now, then next year at normal raspberry time. It seems to spread out the fruiting – no glut to drive you to jam-making with these. These berries on new wood are very large, dark and long, and are completely ignored by the birds, too busy with so many other things. Coal tits have stripped the cluster of purple-blue cones on a Korean pine down to bare sticks, but only the coal tits: the blue-and great-tits they flock with fly to the tree for a moment and off again. There are half a dozen coal-tits working the cones at any one time, flying off with trophies for a moment and returning for more. As unseasonal as raspberries, two swallows above the house field. It's three weeks since I last saw any.

OCTOBER

Every October has at least one day like this: heavy dew, yellow leaves, clear sky. Even contrails across the intense deep blue don't last. There's no wind, at least not at ground level. A red balloon took off from the village at eight this morning and went nowhere until – gas burners roaring intermittently – it lifted much higher, to where you could no longer make out the heads peering down from its basket.

Trees and bushes glitter. Beads of dew flare prismatic red, green, blue in the sun. Midges everywhere. A few late butterflies, Red Admirals, a pair of Speckled Woods and one Comma, bright orange in the light. A tractor and a clatter: the sounds of a roadside hedge being flailed. More tractors busy across the valley while the weather holds: the forecast is for rain and wind.

Dew splits the light in the morning. By late afternoon, it's high cirrus splitting light into sundogs on either side of the sun. While sparks of light in dewdrops are sharp and intense, sundogs in the cirrus are often pearlescent – a hazy brilliance in high ice cloud, with sometimes only a hint of colour. It would be easy not to notice them; I think it's a matter of expectation and knowing where to look – at the same height as the sun when it's quite low, but out to the side by 22 degrees. Ice crystals bend sunlight rays into several arcs and haloes around the sun, but these sundogs are the easiest to spot, occasionally so bright they can dazzle. (It was Barry Lopez who started me looking for parhelia, writing that the most complete set he ever saw was not in the Arctic but over Los Angeles in winter.)

'Our' swallows left early in September, but every so often we see small groups in the late afternoon feeding above the meadow, maybe moving down from Scotland. It's much easier to spot your first swallow of the year than it is your last. But maybe yesterday's, on October 8th, was the last – a single bird fast and low across the garden. Plenty of midges still.

The first migrant passerines flew over on 13th this year heading north, quite low but too fast to tell whether they were fieldfares or redwings or both. There are plenty of holly berries here but they had somewhere else in mind. Plenty of red berries among the red leaves of the guelder rose too, every bush wobbling violently as blackbirds reach for fruit on the ends of twigs.

All year only the odd harsh chortle and screech has reminded you that jays are living their secret life in the woods. Now their white rumps are suddenly visible everywhere as they dash from oak tree to acorn store. Or they'll bob boldly over the lawn, gouge a hole in a spot of significance invisible to the human eye, and ram in an acorn. Accounts vary: a jay will bury two thousand acorns a year, three thousand, five... They certainly find most of them again: if they did not, a dense oak woodland would surround this house. Jays are said to 'remember' where they store their acorns. But all those thousands? There's certainly nothing random about it: a jay fetching its buried breakfast will hop towards the spot, look up, down, around. Hop again, look all round, hop, look and pounce, digging up the acorn in one stab. But what does it look for? If we were down at ground level, one eye looking out from each side of our heads, would we pick two trunks in alignment on one side, the corner of a roof cutting off the top of a birch on another, a gate just obscured by a wall? Is it triangulating its known and favourite landmarks?

There are many lesser migrations going on. This morning, a sparrowhawk sat on a rail in the garden where a female woodpecker had been at work the day before. Neither visited over the summer. Then a small brown bird flashed white underneath as it moved round a trunk: a treecreeper, not seen here since last spring. Small birds are flocking up for winter and they have ritual daily movements of their own, patterns you can anticipate: a mixed flock of nineteen tits flies chaotically up from the wood near the beck, behind the house and then down to the Old Wood at four o'clock each afternoon.

And sometime this month, secretly, a tawny owl returned to his winter roost in the cypress tree near the house. (They don't breed here: they're not builders, so need the floor of a hayloft, or a capacious hollow tree to nest in.) This will be the third winter I know of that an owl has lived here, so a third winter of owl-watching at dusk. Sometimes a 'window' is opened in the tree, a small branch pressed outwards, and an owl stands looking out on the world before swooping down as night falls. All last winter it became an evening vigil, to stand at the window owl-watching, the time predictable by the light. It was by chance we discovered there were two owls in the tree not one, so we know now when owl watching, you keep on watching, in case a second bird follows the first. Exactly when the owl, maybe owls, returned I'm not sure. Earlier this month I called to the geese from the house as the light faded because I hadn't seen them all day. They replied, and the cacophony caused a quiet grey shape to glide from the tree. Yesterday afternoon I walked across the garden, thinking of where to plant bulbs. A long, loud, indignant *hhooo* startled me as I passed the cypress tree: this is the owl's patch now, I must remember, not mine.

I was woken at five in the morning by a soft, sad wail. Not animal and not quite bird. Not the wind; dawn was sliding silently into the east. When I passed the woodburner it called again, sorrowing – some creature trapped in there all night? – after all these years how could one fall down so far? I opened the stove door very slowly, to nothing but last evening's soft wood-ash, undisturbed. *Hoohoohoohooooo:* it was the owl, hooting down the chimney and playing the metal pipe like an echo chamber.

*

Mellow fruitfulness rightly belongs to September, but October 12th has, surprisingly, delivered another small bowl of raspberries from the primocanes, though I'm not altogether sure I like unseasonal fruits. I've always been able to pick Alpine strawberries until the first frost, so there's a large bowl of fruit for tea. *Mists* are October's own.

Frosts soon melt; there's still warmth in the sun. In the still air after frost, a robin follows me round the silent garden. When it lands on the ash tree, even its tiny weight on a twig sends yellow leaves puttering to the ground. A woodpecker's hacking at a rotten elder further down the hedge. Now and again the swish of tyres begins half a mile away, rounds the bends, fades away again. Curious sounds from the cypress tree, a cross between a cough and hoot – the owl dreaming inside its winter tree while I was at the morning's task of picking yellow and black caterpillars off the purple sprouting.

I was less pleased to see six bullfinches back yesterday berrying in the guelder rose and shouted at them, no matter that they're both colourful and declining. If they stay until spring, they'll be stripping flower buds from the apples and plums. Two years ago, they took out every blossom but two on the Victoria.

It's straightforward with caterpillars: a them-or-us battle over the winter brassicas. Then there are squirrels. I've cage-trapped two

this week. The battle with squirrels began over strawberries but it's escalated to a full-scale war in defence of trees. Grey squirrels are able to breed continuously in the mild northern European climate, so there are more of them living at much greater densities than in their native North America. Because of this, they've developed new behaviours, become territorial and will mark out their patch by peeling bark from trees. Not very young trees, and not old trees with thick crusty bark – but trees about fifteen to twenty years old, preferably with smooth bark: beech, sycamore, field maple and horse chestnut are their favourites here. When a tree's ring-barked, it dies.

It's heartbreaking to see piles of bark peelings at the foot of tree after tree. Occasionally we've been able to cut ring-barked branches out of a tree and 'save' the rest, but it's a poor misshapen thing that's left, and open to disease. I'm most sorry to have lost the half dozen chestnuts I'd planted here and there among the oak and ash: at about 30 feet, they'd have been about to flower for the first time.

I wonder what will happen to the millennium woodlands in 2015, when they reach the right size for grey squirrels to de-bark? I wonder what Botanic Gardens do about the grey squirrels their visitors like to see running around? The Royal Society of Foresters is in no doubt about what should be done about them, given the millions of pounds' worth of damage they do – especially to native hardwoods.

Red squirrels lived in the woods here until the 1980s when the greys arrived, vectors for diseases that decimate the reds. Once, when I was sitting very still up a tree above the river, watching the water in case any sunlit ripples on the riverbed turned into fish, a red squirrel ran along the bank, up the tree and over my boot. A red squirrel overwintered in a dinghy we'd stored at the end of the garden ready to paint: the boat never did get done up that year. Since then, I've only seen reds at a feeding station in the Lake District.

Even at the month's end there can be windless days so mild and quiet you can walk outside in shirtsleeves, days so still you can hear the river two hundred foot below the Old Wood. (Geologically speaking, this is a tunnel valley – a wide, gently sloping valley which accommodates its river in a deep trough, originally formed by meltwaters running underneath an ice sheet.) While I was listening to the river and filling the goose troughs with clean water, I was eaten by midges. Tiny spiders were suspended invisibly all over the orchard. I counted a couple of dozen of them on a handspan of deer fence – so many creatures about whose lives I know nothing at all. In the house are moths, equally anonymous, even the cinnamon-coloured ones with orange eyes.

The woodland opposite is russet and bronze. There's green, still, where alders stand and the single red flare of a cherry below Cragg Hall. No clear yellow domes of elm of course.

NOVEMBER

The first real gale on the first of the month, and you open the curtains to an altered world – that opulent oil painting in russets and bronze switched in the night for a charcoal sketch. The leaves are gone, not gradually so you get used to the look of the bare outlines of trees, but all at once. The courgettes are done, shrivelled by the blast. The mint is scorched.

November's a month most of my old notebooks seem to pass over. And there's remarkably little weather lore for November. But that's all right: this feels like a time for stripping away, for getting back to what is simpler, essential. Landscapes do autumn-, not spring-cleaning, though once again wind has had to do the work of frost.

This time last year we *did* have frosts, but the previous two winters passed without any, which seemed very strange. In the garden, I see frost as part of that autumn-cleaning, killing off bugs and diseases. Round here it used to be said you couldn't start your summer veg off until May 15th, and they'd be finished by first frosts on September 15th. This year I'm still picking tomatoes in November.

All the same, a modern frost is another of those things that isn't like it used to be. My god-daughter has never seen windows blanked out by the swirled leaf-patterns of frost. She's never warmed a coin in her hand and pressed it to the glass for a moment to melt a perfect circle of a spy-hole in the white surface. Bedsocks, winceyette pyjamas, stone hot water bottles – all these have passed her by, which makes me wonder whether winters were altogether colder a few decades ago – in the same way that remembered summers of childhood are always sunny – or whether it is, after all, just a matter of better heating and insulation.

There's more sky now, longer horizons. A couple of farm buildings at Cragg Hall across the valley are visible through bare branches. Trees are outlines on which you can read their years of growth. The compost heaps are piled high with what plants have no more use for. Drifts of leaves against fences and walls have been corralled in a wire cage so they can convert themselves into next year's dry, crumbly leafmould.

And now that leaves have gone, I can also see that a hazel fallen across the gulley and on to the path above the beck isn't just fallen but *felled*. I'd scrambled round it in full leaf. Now I see it was skittled over – it and a holly and some smaller hazels – by a flying big-bale. My neighbour made haylage about two months ago on the top of a steeply sloping field above our boundary fence. That boundary runs along a deep gulley. In summer it's almost dry; in winter it's a fast beck. Maybe when they were being carted away, maybe when it dropped out of the baler, one of the huge round bales made off, bounded down the slope gathering speed and took out fence, barbed wire and old hedge to crash into the beck and block it. Anyone idling about in the beck as I sometimes do botanising or birdwatching would have been crushed: a big-bale is big, about 4 foot diameter. *They go hell of a lick,* said Ken when I told him.

It took him most of yesterday to chainsaw the fallen trees and re-fence the gap. The big-bale's still stuck: huge, sodden and immutable. There's no way a tractor and spike can approach from my neighbour's steep side of the gulley nor from mine. The next job will be to cut the net binding from the bale and hope that the force of winter rainwater will tug bits away and down into the river.

The fence was mine; the bale, not. I'm sure my neighbour would have helped with the fence if I'd asked – but his farm is the other side of the river; the land on this side is for hay and winter pasture. It was simpler not to bother him.

Woods usually fence themselves. That is: if you don't want your neighbours' cattle crashing through your wood, it's your job to fence them out, not his. Any map of fields you're buying will have a small **T** drawn on each boundary to show which way responsibility for the fence lies. It doesn't stop disputes. First, there are odd sheep that will jump a fence to be where they think there's better grass and when they've done it once they'll do it again. (One particular Herdwick will break in again just after Christmas from her field over the road; I'll have to drive her into the steep field by the big-bale until her owner collects her. She thinks she should winter down there.) Then there are different ideas about mending fences. I'm of the overkill-school: new posts, a run of American netting, a strand of plain wire and a strand of barbs. The alternative is to stick an old pallet in the gap. Or a branch from a nearby ash tree. Or a wardrobe door. None of which are much of a deterrent to the determined Herdwicks of this world.

In the 1980's, the hedgerow beyond this window where I type was the scene of a boundary war for more than a year. The fence, claimed one neighbour, was fine; it was the other's sheep who were not. The other neighbour claimed the fence inadequate. Solicitor's letters. Insurance claims. A figure betrayed by his red bobble hat shifting about on the far side of the fence behind a holly bush when I got back from work. On this side, another sauntering off, as if just out to take the air. Once, when they were unaware I was at home – such language batted back and forth across the hedge... Not unlike the cock pheasants further along who use the fence to mark their own territories, one either side, ducking heads and rushing at each other, saved from doing or suffering harm by the very fence in question.

I learned my lesson about stock a good while ago when some of my geese migrated downriver. Every day when I got home from work I had to fetch them back, driving them into the river from the same field half a mile away, and wading thigh deep along the riverbed behind them back to my own land and up through the woodland to their own pasture. In the post, a solicitor's letter: *Madam, Unless...*

The most you can hope for in a rural area you weren't born in is to be a good neighbour. Hence my devotion to fencing, no matter how the damage has been done. Hence, too, a permanent holiday in the Lake District for those wandering geese.

*

There's a puddle on the kitchen floor where I've hung my waterproofs. Maybe November goes in for extremes: last year it was proper frost; this year it's rain – 100mm is forecast for the fells today or (a strange sort of forecast) *a possibility of twice that.* Swathes of sky sweep down to blot out the view. No one would go out in this. But farmers need to check stock. Even I've been out to make sure the geese have clean water to wash their eyes in. Thoroughly waterproofed, it wasn't as bad as I expected – though it was noisier, the gale-driven rain rattling against my hood.

Brown water races along ditches. Leaves and twigs quickly form blockages that need a boot under them, before the debris charges off to the river. Mike, ringing from 10 miles downstream yesterday, said great islands of debris as well as whole trees are storming downriver to the Irish Sea. The gurgle, churn and rush of a cleared ditch is so satisfying it's a job everyone offers to do. I've another to check, near a watergate where the beck comes under a fence. I haven't been down there yet: boots sink into the waterlogged ground. Nor have I yet looked at the river, shooting so fast down its rocky bed there will be huge waves and overfalls like those we photographed a few years ago in, yes, November.

Once the leaves had gone, you could see why owls would choose a cypress for a winter roost, thick fronds of evergreen foliage keeping out even driven rain. Now their tree sways and heaves in the gale. How do they hold on in all this? I'm surprised they're in there at all when I think of the shape of the tree, its vertical branches. But every evening at dusk (4.30pm now) they fly out. A couple of days ago, they opened their front door in the foliage, and stood together looking out on the world for half an hour before swooping down over Robins Close Meadow to the Old Wood. One bird's smaller than the other. Tawny yes, but many of the speckled feathers are very pale, white even, on the small male.

That forecast rain was in the end more than 300mm – rain that caused floods across Cumbria and so much damage in Cockermouth, the most rain that has fallen in England since (another one) records began.

In a break in this morning's rain, the wind still strong, I heard a raven. The sky looks empty at first glance: binoculars show you something different. Starlings, a couple of buzzards circling very high, and two ravens, no three, four, is that another? – they're not easy to count as they're so fast, gliding, rolling, plummeting, climbing. Maybe this is a whole family of them. An unkindness of ravens? Unkind itself, this collective noun: what's going on out there is more of an exuberance, a showing-off, a circus.

A week after its floods, Cumbria had one lovely day, cold and bright, the sky deep blue behind snow-covered tops, old bracken on the valley sides bright russet in the sun. Early in the morning, the car park in Ambleside was almost full: there must have been a hundred people lacing their boots.

On the last day of the month, a few birch trees still sport a small skull cap of yellow leaves. A few alders hang on to a dowdy wrap of shrivelling leaves: they neither colour nor drop, just fade from dull green to khaki; let go a few at a time.

THE

ANATOMY

OF

LEAVES

DECEMBER

If months had flags, December's would be blue and white and charcoal. I opened the curtains on its first day to clear sky and white rag on the ground, overnight cold doffing the remaining gold from the birch and stripping the alder, revealing not bare twigs but next season's catkins already well-formed and pink-tinged.

Winter highs and their still air are wonderful if you live on top of a hill. Up here, grass starts to show green again from sun-up. In the valley bottoms, frosts don't clear. Crystals build overnight on top of crystals, so that after a few days, white spikes sprout along the tops of stone walls. Roofs hold their white coating all day down there; it looks a cold place to live.

Skies are better on top of a hill. Sometimes classic clear blue, setting off shining silver birch trunks and their dark red filigree of twigs, sometimes shading from light blue in the east, darker overhead and away to pale celadon in the west that persists behind a few stray raspberry clouds at sunset. When there's a band of cloud round high pressure, you can see all of it, arcing up from the moor and out to sea. Yesterday a line of lens-shaped clouds came off the moor at sunrise, towing behind it a narrow band of flocculations that slowly widened as it crossed towards the sea. Sometimes the contrail of an transatlantic flight from Manchester casts a straight-line shadow on cloud below it.

In cold still air, sound travels: children's voices which I thought were just beyond the garden hedge came from Cowkins, half a mile away. Sunday morning, it was shots you could hear – not the predictable pop-pop of a clay shoot down in the field opposite the pub, but the stuttering random fusillades of a shoot on Perry Moor: pheasants. This last few years, a different breed of pheasants has been introduced. The plump bronze-bodied, purple-headed birds we're used to aren't apparently much fun to shoot, being too idle to get off the ground and fly, intent as they are on suicide by motor vehicle. The birds now bred for shooting are smaller, the cock birds almost black. They're *flighty*, I'm told. Terry complains of what he calls *the fancy Italian ones* that, when you let them out of the breeding pens, won't stay put; you have to chase around after them, round them up for their feed. The two types interbreed of course, but there seem plenty of suicidal ones still with us.

Frozen ground can be hard enough for tractors to drive over where they would otherwise sink. When the ground's frozen long enough to bear the weight of tractor and tank, a lot of slurry gets spread. Smells travel through still air as well as sound. Today, it seems best not to hang my washing outdoors.

*

In the same way you never see the last few swallows leave, you never see the last few holly berries disappear. There was an inch of snow when I took the secateurs round the hedgerows to cut Christmas greenery – not a single berry to be found. Even the tree outside my study window was plain green; even the *Ilex bacciflava* by the greenhouse, its yellow berries usually having no appeal to birds, had been stripped. We're having an old-fashioned cold spell, the temperature not rising above zero, with that dull yellow daylight that snow clouds create. A friend who lives 100 feet higher was marooned yesterday, and the lazy snowflakes falling intermittently today are going to seal us into the same white silence. Later, I'll take our empty milk bottles to the cattlegrid. The milkman will be able to get that far at least along a gritted road.

Everything takes longer in this weather, needs planning. Hat, coat, gloves and boots even to re-supply the bird table, two robins so intent on preventing the other from feeding that they eat nothing, a hell-for-leather flurry of wings and feathers churning up dry snow on the ground beneath the table, while a shy dunnock takes advantage of their hostilities to gulp seed after seed. The woodpeckers take turns on the peanuts; they hang there after feeding, keeping off smaller birds until their partner appears on the top twig of an ash tree in the hedge. Then they change places. The cold drove even long-tailed tits from the woods to the feeder, a whole flock of them landing on it to make a single wriggling creature hanging there, black and white tails sticking out at all angles.

Thick snows can seem all inconvenience, but each fresh fall reminds you it can be transformative too, reflecting back the blue of a cleared sky or the gold of dawn. It transforms north-facing woodlands on the steeply sloping side of the valley more than anywhere. I look across to those woods every day, their trees a heaped cumulus of greens in summer and purple-red twigs in winter. Only under a heavy snowfall do you see the woodland floor, how steeply it plunges down to the river. Tree trunks are bundles of black lines on a white ground now, extraordinarily tall and thin reaching for the light. At one time – maybe as recently as 80 years ago to judge by some of the trunks – the woodlands would have been worked, thinned and coppiced, stands of elm alternating with hazel coppice and all with enough light and air around them to grow well. Now they're overcrowded, spindly, re-seeded by sycamore and birch. This last few years holly has sprung up everywhere, and made it to about a foot high without being eaten off by hares and deer. Now it's the only green stuff above the snow, I expect to find much of it grazed.

*

Some short periods of sun have shifted the worst snow from the villages and gardens and gritted roads, but shade and higher ground remain snowbound. Un-treated roads are so slippery you can't even walk on them. Grey stone villages strike the eye as immensely colourful and intricately patterned after all this long period of gently undulating snow. There seems too much to look at.

This last day of the month is also the last of the decade, notable for a blue moon as well as a lunar eclipse, at least a partial one. A high layer of cloud in the afternoon made me expect it would pass unseen, just another night strangely lit by snow reflections. But cloud drifted away south on an icy northern airstream, and a radiant moon lifted up through the birch trees, before a little patch lower right was nibbled away by the evening's eclipse for an hour. The cold layered itself inside our clothes. We were glad to run back indoors to work out how eclipses happen – as I have to every time – on the kitchen table, with an orange for the sun, an onion for earth and (whatever comes to hand) a grape for the moon.

JANUARY

Winters, we've been complaining for years, *are not what they used to be*. Sledges and cross country skis were abandoned somewhere under the eaves in the attic long ago. But the winter of 2009/10 is turning into the old-fashioned sort. The fields are hard frozen underfoot. Lower slopes untouched by sun retain their ten day old snow, so hard now that it can bear weight – or else hold you momentarily then collapse and drop you. The pond's solid, with a layer of new snow on top.

On deep frozen snow, footprints crunch loudly. Creatures must be able to hear us coming from a field away, yet all the same wait until the very last minute to move off – pheasants are good at startling you whatever the weather, but a woodcock was even more of a surprise. Few prints appear on deep snow that's accompanied by extreme cold. Even four days after the freeze that started early in the month, most of the Goose Field was unmarked. Deer had been out and about on all that expanse of possibilities yet their slots were in straight lines exactly where the footpaths are. A fox had been more innovative, up from the Old Wood, over the banking at the south side of the pond and straight out to the middle of the ice, where it executed two tight circles, a scuffle, and then back to the edge where a land drain runs into the pond and there's the merest drop of fresh water. There wasn't the slightest movement in the ice when I stood on it, slowly giving it more and more of my weight.

Up in the house field, snow preserved evidence: a light orange mark on the snow every few feet, drag marks, scuffs down to bushes beside the beck. The corpse had been left neat and tidy; the fox had cut off the head and neck. And it must have happened in daylight, while I was around; I'd counted the flock a few hours before, mid-morning. (A count is automatic; you do it without thinking every time you look at a flock – even when you come across a field full of wild greylags on South Uist.) For once I left the corpse, thinking the fox would be back again, and better that than lose another bird.

The owl, too, changed its routine in the cold, parting the branches of its cypress roost and looking out just after midday, then swooping off down to the wood.

Another snowfall this morning is one of the most beautiful I've seen here. Falling after weeks of frost, snow now sticks to even the smallest twigs. Birch trees with their thin high tracery are the most exquisitely transformed. The fields are flat white, brighter than the snow-freighted sky. Woodland across the valley is light grey. The gable end of the distant farm on the skyline stands out starkly now, triangular, the only dark thing in a white landscape.

In all this white, the woodpecker's vermillion undertail coverts and scarlet nape are startling. There are tiny flashes of red in the other Januaries too, the damp, drear ones with dead leaves and broken trees. What I took to be a scarlet sweet wrapper among leaf litter in the Old Wood turned out to be three bowl-shaped fungi, *Sarcoscyphus coccinea* when I looked them up, each smaller than a thumbnail. I'd expected they'd be one of those fungi with telling old names like Cramp-balls and Plums-and-custard, but my reference book gave none, so I made do with that deathly carmine wine cup. Later, I found it in the Collins' *New Naturalist* series among the woodland fungi, referred to as *not-much-studied* – but so attractive *it is often used with moss* (this was written in 1953) *as a table decoration.*

Buff and grey no longer camouflage against a white background. A covey of ten red-legged partridges, all dressed up with striped black bibs and fan-patterned party frocks, scuffle snow under a hedgerow for something to pluck at. A blue-tit is bluer and yellower than I'd thought. Perhaps white light reflecting back from snow intensifies colours.

A snow-plough went along the road this morning clearing a route to the school on the fells, but more snow's fallen since. The morning has gone to shovelling enough of a path to fetch in logs. There'll be no post, no going out with a car. Next there'll be hot water to carry out in buckets for the geese, their troughs to look for under the snow so they can be fed. One forgets the nuisance value of 'real' winters, and now we've got one, wish it would stop.

By 7th January, the low temperatures are even lower: at ten o'clock, we've only warmed up to *minus* 9°C. Water spilled against the house wall as we filled buckets for the geese with a pipe rigged up through the kitchen window froze on the stone. Three-inch tubes of ice, capped with red foil, reared up from the milk bottles I fetched from the cattle grid, even though I'd left a box for Norman to put them in. Every leaf and green stem on the large-leaved ivy up the garden fence has disappeared – their prints in the snow tell us deer were hungry enough for this usually unpalatable greenery. I'm beginning to wonder what will survive and what will be lost in the garden; many plants here haven't been exposed to this degree of cold before. Though 'old-fashioned' plants should be fine about the cold. Certainly dormant fruit trees will be. We were surprised how friable the soil was under a thin icy crust when we scraped back the snow blanket to dig parsnips. We covered the rest over again with snow.

Two more nights of extraordinary cold, and the river's frozen over. You can find the odd pool of clear water where the channel is both fast and deep, but for most of the stretch I walked you can't exactly tell where the beach ends and water starts. The pools are six inches lower than the ice shelf: the river level must have fallen since it froze. Stones on the beach have grown spikes of ice on top of their snow; spikes beget spikes, so little fans of ice thrust upwards in every direction. Animal prints wander on to the ice and cross over – not a risk I wanted to take.

I had done, seven years before, to rescue a new gander stuck on the frozen pond. The rest of the flock had returned at the end of the day, but he was trapped on the ice having done the splits. (He was a heavier bird than those I'd bred myself, so maybe that was why.) There seemed nothing for it but to crash in and grab him. The icy water hurt. I carried him the two fields back home. He was bandy-legged for a day or two, but came to no harm. I didn't either, but the extreme cold of the water and wet clothes needed a long while in a hot bath to leave me.

Meantime, on with old jumpers smelling of their years with mothballs. Can it really only have been three years ago we had no frost at all except for 3 days in November? In the mild winters we've got used to, snow stays up on the fells. The river foams up, falls back, slews stones about, foams up. The land holds water, holds footprints and grass yellows. Sometimes after heavy rain, you can hear an old stone land drain underground gurgling and chuckling to itself. Ditches have to be unblocked of dead leaves. In 1999 the first frost came on 9th January after weeks of mild weather, though none of that mildness was pleasant – windy enough to bring down more trees and power lines, and wet enough for small floods over most local roads. Windy enough too to take out the timbers of the barn on the skyline. Its familiar skeletal ribs fell in, leaving a new view : what was left standing, square, slabby and lifeless.

That was the year what I thought of as 'a stoat in half-ermine' surveyed the garden: white tail, white forelegs and more white than usual spread across its belly. This pied winter coat must have been caused by a cold period triggering the development of white hairs during the start of the autumn moult, and then a milder spell triggering patches of brown hairs. A couple of years before that we'd had one in full ermine – visible half a field away against grass, an obvious meal for a passing raptor. I see them much more rarely now; not once in the past year. (Only a couple of weeks after writing this, an ermine crossed in front of the car, a shining white ripple disappearing into the hedge bottom.)

Wind and wet characterise most Januaries here. The highest gust we've ever had was in January, in 1991. There's a list of gusts pinned up by the anemometer dial: all the strongest are in January. The noise of 100km/h on 7 Jan 2005 was frightening. Three years ago, 78km/h with a twist of north in it blew down a Scots pine in the orchard. The tree was only about fifteen years old, but so big when it was down it seemed like a creature the size of a blue whale slumbering on the grass, sea-green fur rippling in the last of the breeze. The trunk had split at shoulder height, and the split ran right down into the ground. You could put your hand down into the root. The smell of pine didn't wash off.

There are no gusts on the list for this January; it has turned dank. With no wind to blow them away, tell-tale fragments of flower buds cover the ground under the bullace trees. Those trees are supporting six bullfinches this year. There will only be a few flowers and fruits at the very ends of twigs. I've seen only one bullfinch-free crop, the weighted branches so low they blocked the path. The cold has also brought a never-before nuthatch to the feeder, a vicious dagger-headed torpedo which chisels nuts down to a size it can wrest through the wire. Other small birds fly off at its approach: this is not a companionable feeder. It, in turn, gives way to the woodpeckers.

This was the coldest January (in the north) for more than 24 years. But there was more sun and far, far less rain than usual – only about half the usual amount, so we can walk on the land without mud squelching over the tops of our boots; it makes all the work so much easier. Has the risk of heavy snow passed? Can we start on winter hedge-laying without worrying a build-up could weigh down the low laid branches and break the slender strip of bark connecting them to their rootstocks? The 'window' for hedging is short: after snow and ice, but well before bud burst. It's the task that turns the corner towards spring.

At the mild month end on the last day of the 20th century, a pipistrelle flittered down from the roof and across to the Little Wood. Not a mild ending to the month this year, but a bright one. I got out of bed in the middle of the night thinking it was nearly daylight. It was 4am, and such strong moonlight that I thought I could just begin to make out colour. A full moon perigee – as close as it comes.

Snowdrops in the old hedgerows are up regardless. As ever.

TRACE

Snowdrop

Doubles. Along the bank under the old hedgerow. Tiny white spears among last year's dead leaves. Slender on cold days, then one day sun and suddenly they are here, the flowers fattened, petals wide. Their sweet, strong scent.

The three outer petals are long and plain. They curve down and in. In sun, they stretch apart so between them you can see three short inner petals, each with a small green horseshoe-mark at its edge. Turn up the flower, and inside these petals – what? a dozen more cram round each other, green-striped. Except few seem regular like this: some flowers have four outer petals and fewer inner ones; some have erratic inner petals, pure white and long.

Every year, the surprise of them, though they've been here far longer than me, a trace of some forgotten garden.

Pipe stem

A piece of clay pipe stem in the vegetable garden. Another. Over the years I've collected more than a hundred such. And nine broken pipe bowls, most of them plain, but one a little larger than the others and patterned with stripes and two rows of leaves. To begin with, it seemed every forkful of earth turned up another treasure.

But only in the vegetable garden. Though it's no accident that the vegetable garden is where it is, west of the house: when we ploughed the acre of meadow that was to be made into a garden with lawns and shrubs and a kitchen garden, one square of soil in the corner was completely different from the rest: dark and crumbly. The rest was poor, sticky clay. Yellowish. It wouldn't have produced good crops. So the kitchen garden had to be away from the house, on that good soil. The farmer who'd sold the land agreed it was odd, he'd noticed he'd always had more hay out of that corner than anywhere else.

Only years of digging and manuring could have changed the nature of the soil so much. Imagine a man digging after his day's work, smoking his clay pipe, snapping it, then treading it in, another trace of life lived here. He takes a new white pipe from his pocket and lights up.

Snowdrop and pipe stem and mine

Even more snowdrops cover another bank on the steep roadside half a mile downhill – the same type, chaotic doubles. Between here and there is an old farmhouse: no snowdrops there.

This other snowdrop bank runs along the back garden of a late Victorian house, but before that was built, a row of miners' cottages fronted the road. And a miner lived here, in this house, too. At least that's how James Taylor described himself to the first census. The enumerator referred to the place Moor End – which it was in 1841, the broad swathe between holly hedges in front of the building still unenclosed land leading on to a moor.

By the time of that census, James was over fifty. He'd been here some years, baptising a child in the parish in 1824. I'll say he came here from the village where he was born, half a day's walk away, because there was work in the mines – the 1820s and 1830s were the busiest time in the small pits round here – and less and less work on the land in that restless migratory time, as machines took over agricultural work.

There are dozens of disused mines all over the moors – nothing industrial, no deep shaft mines: the seams were only a foot or so thick – often bell-pits, with a short shaft down to the seam, and the hole widened out at the bottom as far as was safe. There'd been a mine quarter of a mile east of here on the common, where James may have started out, but it was filled in by 1834. There was a colliery with a proper shaft and tunnels a mile to the north, but – because of those shared snowdrops – I'll have James keep company with the miners from the row of cottages down the hill, working in the smaller pits on the moor to the south. James could be down there with them in ten minutes. They'd only to cross the river, and climb through the steep woods at the other side to be at the pits.

James didn't only plant double snowdrops round his home; they're followed by daffodils on the bank too – the small native pale ones, *Narcissus lobularis*, but in their double form, *flore pleno*, their long trumpets filled with petals, sometimes greenish not just pale yellow. Miners I knew a century and a half later were all gardeners, too, and with a penchant for doubles – as if the frill and froth of the flowers were some sort of counter to the dark and the dust of their working life. Horace, who had two allotments, bred an orange-yellow double begonia that was named for his niece. His wife Nelly wanted him to go gardening after the war, saying people would always need gardeners. But Horace loved it down the mine, and wouldn't leave. He said people would always need coal. I hear James saying the same to his wife, when he moved away from the Lune and into the hills: *People will always need coal. There'll always be work up there.*

*

James steps outside on to cobbles. A couple of strides and he's on unenclosed land that leads up to the common. (Some of the hedges I see now, standing in the same place, haven't been planted yet.) As he turns downhill towards the hamlet where the miners live, neat oblongs of land have been enclosed on both sides of the track. Stone drains have been laid every few yards in these fields, drawing the land's wetness away to the River Hindburn south of the track and to Clearbeck on the north side. The field boundaries are well-built cops: double low stone walls, back-filled with soil from ditches dug alongside them, and planted with whitethorn or blackthorn. They're impenetrable. In the winters, he speaks to men at work all along them. They split the longest, strong uprights at the base and lay them low to the ground, pinning them in by short stakes cut from the hedge. New growth shoots up from the base, to be laid in turn a few years later when the old, now dead, liggers are taken out – work only done these days on a grant, or out of sentiment. James would be shocked at hedges now: fruits and new growth machine-flailed in autumn, gappy at the bottom, the stonework just a mossy mound; some let go altogether into malformed trees and bushes, then backed up with posts, American netting and barbs.

He'd puzzle at what comes up in the hay meadows now. What he sees – and smells – over the cops in spring as he walks down the hill are waves of white and yellow and pink shading into each other. Grasses are the least of it. Dog daisies near the edge, then buttercups, ladies fingers, tormentil, hayrattle, self-heal, burdock, eyebright, the pink or white pyramids of orchids, a hundred or so of them to a square yard – yes, flowers as dense as that: what he simply takes for granted, just part of the natural flow of seasonal change, *we* marvel at. Only one small field, an acre or so, would feel familiar to him still. Just beyond where the row of miners' cottages were at the bottom of the hill, a quirk of woodland and walls and a curve in the beck has kept machinery (and therefore fertiliser) out. We call it a *Site of Special Scientific Interest*. But the footpath James would have taken if he walked on further to the village downstream still runs through it; you can stand where he stood, looking down, and time-travel, amazed.

As amazed as he and his friends would be to walk up through today's woods to the mines. It would seem to them as if some unimaginable disaster had happened. Not just that the elms have disappeared, though that would be curious – what would strike them first is the silence, the woods no longer full of the sound of work. Then: the neglect, windblows left to rot, coppice outgrown, no strong timber, no rotations, nothing maintained.

They're used to greetings and conversations as they walk up through the woods. They're used to the smoke from charcoal burners' stacks. In June, oak-peeling is underway for the tanners. In colder months, poles are cut from the large coppiced elms for the bobbin mill behind the miners' houses and the thick stands of hazel wands along the edges of the woods are being coppiced for the basket makers' rims, who also want good taws of peeled oak to boil, ready for weaving into their swills. The wheelwright wants ash; the cloggers, alder; the joiners, the best of everything. Carefully harvested woods are fundamental to the industries that sustain every aspect of the life these men know. Every piece of timber is measured and accounted for. Their own work depends on the woodland – for their pick-shafts, for corves to carry the coal, for the turn-tree to lift corves to the surface.

Ancient Semi-Natural Woodland we call these steep valley sides, as if to preserve something of value. But what was of value is replaced largely by rotting birch and spindly sycamore. Of all the changes to the landscape, I think this is the one that James would find most incomprehensible.

I see James as a church-goer. He rents this house from the Reverend Richard Skirrow, and with it a small patch of land fenced off in a corner of the meadow – a 'garden' on the parish Tithe Map of 1848. The house is a two-storey affair, built on the end of an outbarn belonging to the adjacent farm, which Reverend Skirrow rents out separately. At some point the cottage has been improved, with a stone lintel and stone starts round a new door on the north side. (The barn has been altered too: its roof, and its arch, raised by three foot.) I'm guessing the alterations are done when the house is let separately from the barn and rest of the farm, that is, when James becomes the tenant. The original doorway with wooden lintels on the north west corner is blocked up.

(We un-blocked it. It's our back door. Anyone over 5'6" has to duck. Underneath the stone flags, we found a George III penny, dating that floor to the 1760s or later and The New Improvements which carved fields and new farms from the moor.)

Here is a kitchen and back kitchen, with an easy ladder from the back kitchen to the upstairs floor. Oak beams and joists; oak floorboards. It's a good house, with an upstairs fireplace, though you'll catch your head on the main roof truss upstairs until you're used to it.

When James's wife steps out, she turns the opposite way from him, towards the moor. Her pullen are already out on common land. The muddy track dips for a hundred yards, then she takes a path northwards another fifty yards to the well. A good house it may be, but the uphill return with the water's wearying. There's a water butt by her door though: stone corbels support a wide wooden gutter on one side of the roof. (As late as 1942, the wartime farm survey shows 'roofwater' was still the main water-source here.) Like James, Betty meets neighbours as she goes – there's always someone coming and going on the common land and the well also serves a farm and cottages further along the enclosed land; the cottagers are hatters, always needing water for their trade. Washing? That has to wait for warm days, when Betty can make her way down the pack road that passes near the house and winds down through the woods to the river. She spreads her washing to dry on the furze near the house. Occasional weekend walkers use Betty's paths today, but they pause and check their maps, the paths grown-over and invisible now.

Pouring my small box of treasures dug from the garden on to the kitchen table, I see it like this: James living here all those years, smoking out in the garden, perhaps, but also sitting with his pipe by the fire. When it breaks, he tosses the pieces into a bucket which already has in it cabbage leaves for the midden, and an iron button, useless with its loop snapped off. There's no such thing as waste. Everything goes to the midden, rots down, is worked into the soil.

So here also are five clay marbles James's children once played with. Here are pieces of Betty's pots, yes some of that brown-on-brown striped local earthenware, and the neck of a stoneware jar, but also the handle from her best tureen, glazed white china with a row of small black leaves round the outside. How she regretted the knob breaking off that lid, too. Only one thing is entire: a tiny stoneware bottle, two and a half inches high, and small enough to slip through the tines of a garden fork. It could only have been used for medicine.

James fetched it for her, his Betty. As he fetched her the first snowdrops along with potatoes from his pie at the end of the garden, as he fetched bunches of double daffs he grew for her in the lean days of spring when they depended on her skill at making oatcakes and preserving, as much as on his at growing vegetables. He'd planted bullace and damson into the hedgerows which sheltered the snowdrops. Betty always had preserves and vinegars in store in the back kitchen.

She was younger by five years than him. He loved her: why else would he have been growing double daffs but to hand her a riot of spring, of exuberance, of celebration? They had strong children, survivors, chattering barefoot down the rough stone on the hill after their father, then turning north away from the river and up to the school. In 1841, when James was already over fifty, their twenty-year-old son James was still living with them, and fifteen-year-old William. Ann (eleven) was at school. Mary (thirteen) was looking after four-year old Arthur, their last child: Betty was forty-five. Maybe William went to work with his father, one of the boys pulling corves of coal out of the mines, knees padded with straw as he crawled along.

James outlived his way of life: the rural industries petered out; the land he stepped out on was no longer common; there was no more to-and-fro outside his door. He outlived his landlord. The property had passed to Rev. Skirrow's daughter Margaret by the time of those last 1858 enclosures. James outlived his wife: by 1861 she was dead and the children had left home – though an older son, Richard, born in 1811, was here with him on census night. Homeless? workless? or here to care for his father, then seventy-two and describing himself as an 'agricultural labourer', perhaps odd-jobbing at the farm on land he knew so well after living on it, walking it, and watching it for forty years. Longer, just, than I've lived here.

FIRESIDE

Feet on the fender, James and I sit in his/my kitchen, a jug of damson gin between us. (Actually, it's more his kitchen than mine: the coal is local shaley stuff that smoulders and sizzles and blows tar bubbles.) We're comparing maps. His is the 1865 – what I call the Old Series Ordnance Survey – black and white, but so intricately engraved that you can see immediately how the land rises from steep valleys, undulates and levels to the moors. Better than you can on my Landranger.

What strikes him is what's changed: the railway's gone. He can't get over that what altered his world so profoundly could simply disappear. It was the railway that put him out of work, bringing cheap coal from pits that could be worked by machine. It put the hatters in the next cottage along out of work, and the nailmakers in the village, and the miller: one by one, all the small rural industries closed down. And then young people left on the trains because there was no work.

I tell him I remember the Cat and Rat railway bridge a few miles down the line from here being dismantled so the road could be straightened. His *Little North Western Railway* lasted less than

120 years, *sleepers uplifted* in 1967.

What strikes *me* is how little has changed apart from that black line on the map that once curved away south-west down the Lune Valley. I reckon James and I could swap maps and walk each other's landscapes. We know our way along the same bridleways and single-track roads. We've both walked the dense network of footpaths which run from farm to church, from farm to school, and farm to farm. The same high stone walls mark the boundary between the rushes of rough moorland grazing and lower pasture. The steep gills remain wooded. The same buildings are named, though the tiny black oblong where we sit is un-named on both maps. A few small field barns have fallen into heaps of stone; one hamlet is smaller; another, near the school, slightly bigger.

What changes there are, are not visible in the broad brushstrokes of this landscape but in its detail. The same band of upland farmsteads rings the moor. But only a few of these today are working farms: one family will run the acreage that used to support several. Many of the old farms and their barns and outbuildings are 'conversions' – one nearby collection of farm buildings is now ten separate dwellings, with extensions, small gardens and 4 x 4s.

Field patterns are unchanged, though here and there a hedgerow has disappeared, its line marked by a row of old oaks and stones from the cop. James has never seen early summer fields this colour, this vivid emerald. In fact pasture's altogether a mystery – nothing but grass. Only that one small Site of Special Scientific Interest looks 'normal' to him in its variety of grasses and herbs and wildflowers.

Most of the hedgerows need netting to make them stockproof but here and there James finds a hedge laid in the traditional way, even if its seasonal growth is controlled by mechanical flail. On several larger farms new hedges have been planted, the young plants wrapped in plastic spirals to keep off rabbits and browsing deer. *Deer?* James shakes his head, unsure whether to believe me. We talk about the Old Wood and how many people would have worked it: a couple of dozen we think, the wood filled with their talk and clatter and smoke, keeping shy deer away. When people abandoned the woods, the deer moved in. And thrived.

Managed and replanted hedgerows cost much more than post and netting, but they're usually part of the contract a landowner has for his grant from the Countryside Stewardship Scheme. Acronyms chart a radical shift of values even through the time I've lived here, the old Min of Ag giving way to MAFF and then DEFRA. Rather than to agriculture, politics and money now address themselves to 'rural affairs' – all kinds of tourist and sporting activities. To every farm, its tea shop. Stewardship grants place a high value on appearances, even if they are couched in the language of biodiversity: there are grants for re-planting hedges, grants for grazing moorland with older and hardier (and otherwise less profitable) breeds of cattle to reduce the spread of gorse and scrub, grants for wildflowers (at least in modest strips round the edges of fields). 'Pays more to grow weeds and wildflowers / these days than milk cows' are lines from a poem I wrote a few years ago – but I didn't invent them; it's a common enough complaint among the generation who started work on the land in order to produce food. This winter I was asked by a neighbour to identify a couple of hedgerow trees before a hedge was laid; forty years ago I was asked to look at sheets of figures about milk-yield and butterfat percentages and work out the best bull to use.

Today's landscape is familiar to James in its broad outlines because it is his nineteenth century landscape we've fixed on as the ideal. Yet this landscape we're so keen to preserve is a recent one. Before the early eighteenth century, the fields and hedgerows that surround us didn't exist: this was moorland – boggy, rushy, bristling with gorse – used as common grazing land in the summer. The process of pulling fields out of such unlikely land has always astonished me: impossible-seeming work without industrial machinery. Yet over this last two years, I've watched Martin, a young man in his twenties, come down the track to revive a hillside further on that had been let run back to scrub. After his day's work on a farm, at weekends, on summer evenings, he's digging, felling, clearing, burning. He checks his ewes. He runs up the land's steep slope. His first field. (Ken's only comment: *He's enjoying himself.*) It's as if I'm looking at the hope, the attachment to land, that first settled this place.

Suppose James and I, our feet on the fender, shift along a bit and make room for young Martin to join us from the future. What will he tell us? That he does, indeed, now run a farming 'theme park' for tourists from the towns and his main worry is carparking? That the shaley 12" coal seams James used to work were a sign of something big – there's a dual carriageway up the valley to service the five pumping stations in the parish, the whole region subject to fracking to keep the carbon economy alive a few more years? Or that the years I wrote about were the last which had predictable seasons: winters became colder and colder for longer periods, and it was just too expensive to keep milk cows indoors for so long and most of the young folk have moved south?

Six feet on the fender, we stare into the flames.

List of Photographs

Acknowledgements

Thanks are due to the editors of journals and books who published early versions of some of these essays in *Earthlines*, *The North*, *Contourlines* (Magdalene College and Salt Publishing) and *Mostly Truthful* (Flax Books).

The staff of Bowland AONB have been hospitable and encouraging, and I'm grateful to Sandra Silk for arranging for me to view their photographic archive, as well as to Graham Cooper for the cover image and to Jon Brook for digital copies of my gelatin silver prints.

My special thanks go to Ken for making working days such pleasure, and to Mike – astute critic and unfailing friend.

J.R.